Everyday Life in Medieval Times

The EVERYDAY LIFE series is one of the
best known and most respected of all
historical works, giving detailed insight
into the background life of a particular
period. This edition provides an invaluable
and vivid picture of the everyday life in
Medieval times from the reign of
Charlemagne to the coming of the
Renaissance.

Marjorie Rowling investigates the Middle
Ages; the people who lived in it; what they
did and how they conducted their affairs;
and we learn of their work and their
homes, of their hopes and fears.

Other EVERYDAY LIFE Books

and published by Carousel Books

MARJORIE ROWLING

EVERYDAY LIFE IN MEDIEVAL TIMES

Drawings by John Mansbridge

CAROUSEL EDITOR: ANNE WOOD

CAROUSEL BOOKS
A DIVISION OF TRANSWORLD PUBLISHERS LTD
A NATIONAL GENERAL COMPANY

To Maurice

EVERYDAY LIFE IN MEDIEVAL TIMES
A CAROUSEL BOOK o 552 54029 3

Originally published in Great Britain
by B. T. Batsford Ltd.

PRINTING HISTORY
Batsford edition published 1968
Batsford edition reprinted 1969
Carousel edition published 1973

Carousel Books are published by
Transworld Publishers Ltd., Cavendish House,
57–59 Uxbridge Road, Ealing, London W.5 5SA.

Made and printed in Great Britain by
C. Nicholls & Company Ltd.

CONTENTS

1 · Street scene, showing a building being demolished and other activities

From the fifteenth-century manuscript of Valerius Maximus

THE ILLUSTRATIONS

ACKNOWLEDGMENT

To Mr J. J. Bagley of the University of Liverpool, to Dr J. M. W. Bean of the University of Manchester, and to Dr N. B. Lewis, Emeritus Professor of Medieval History at the University of Sheffield, who generously read and helpfully criticised the book in typescript, the author is particularly indebted.

The author and publishers wish to thank the following authors and publishers for permission to use the quotations that appear in this book:
C. C. Swinton Bland, *The Autobiography of Guibert, Abbot of Nogent-sous-Coucy* (Routledge and Kegan Paul Ltd) p. 72; Bryce Lyon (editor), *The High Middle Ages* (University of California Press) p. 246; Iris Origo, *The Merchant of Prato* (Jonathan Cape Ltd) pp. 53 and 56; Helen Waddell, *Medieval Latin Lyrics* (Constable and Co. Ltd) p. 42; Helen Waddell, *The Wandering Scholars* (Constable and Co. Ltd) pp. 97, 138, 141, 187 and 189.

The author and publishers also wish to thank the following for permission to reproduce the illustrations appearing in this book: Aachen Cathedral Treasury for fig. 7; The Trustees of the British Museum for figs. 8, 27 and 46; J. E. Bulloz, Paris for figs. 44 and 76; A. F. Kersting F.R.P.S. for fig. 45; the Mansell Collection for figs. 26, 28, 36, 55 and 75; Foto Ann Munchow for fig. 7; the Bodleian Library, Oxford for fig. 86*; the Bibliothèque Nationale, Paris for figs. 1 and 77; Thames and Hudson Ltd for figs. 20, 58, 59, 61, 63, 64, 66 and 80, taken from *The Flowering of the Middle Ages* (ed. Joan Evans); *The Radio Times* Hulton Picture Library for fig. 9; the Victoria and Albert Museum for fig. 35. The President and Fellows of Corpus Christi College, Oxford, for figs. 56 and 57 which are from Ms CCC 157.

* Published on colour filmstrip 161 C Marco Polo, Bodleian Ms Bodley, Folio 218.

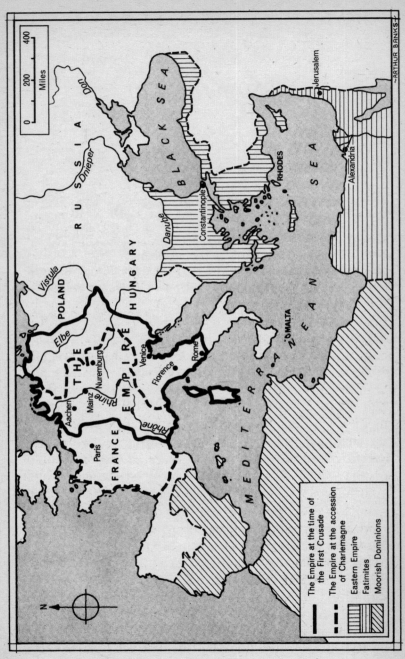

2 Europe at the time of the First Crusade in 1095

1

CHARLEMAGNE AND SOCIETY

IN the year A.D. 814, within the palace he had built at Aachen, the Emperor Charles the Great—Charle-magne—died. Not long after, a monk of Bobbio, in Italy, put into the words of a lament the sense of fear and loss which 'Franks, Romans and all Christian folk' felt on the death of so great a warrior and ruler: 'Woe is me! We are plunged into mourning and overcome by grief. . . . Francia which has passed through such dire catastrophes has never borne so great a sorrow as that of committing to his grave at Aachen the august and eloquent Charles.' Charlemagne soon became a legend, and was placed as a universal hero, along with Abraham and Caesar, among the Nine Worthies revered in medieval times. But the great emperor, illuminated by the artificial roseate glow of romance, can well stand scrutiny beneath the clearer, more revealing light of history. There he is shown as laying foundations which —although some of the edifices reared upon them may have been temporarily destroyed—remained as the solid basis for much that became part of the very fabric of medieval Europe.

In every facet of life—territorial, economic, educa-tional, political, cultural, ecclesiastical and social—something at least of Charles' acts and ideals lived on. Indeed the changes he brought about justify us in referring to his times as 'the Age of Charlemagne', for he not only brought order—at least for a time—to a

3   Statuette probably of
          Charlemagne

chaotic and semi-bar-
barous Europe, but re-
vived the late Roman
ideal of an empire that
was also a Christian
society. He encouraged
the preservation of the
ancient classical heri-
tage, the education and
reform of the clergy and
the provision of monastic
and cathedral schools, as
well as giving western
Europe a coinage—that
of pounds, shillings and
pence—which is still (in
1968) used in Britain.
In addition, Charle-
magne's development
of the lord-man relation-
ship, allied with a system
of land tenure which linked vassal to lord by an oath
of fidelity, became the basis for the later feudal organisation of society. Finally, Charlemagne's achievements and personality impressed not only his own age
but became the centre of a myth and of hero worship in
later centuries. Indeed the name of Charlemagne can
stir the imagination even after a lapse of eleven
hundred years.

What type of man then, was Charlemagne? Certainly no plaster saint, but as passionate, lustful and
cruel as many of his contemporaries. His religion was
mainly one of outward observance, without much
spiritual depth. His greatest asset—perhaps the secret
of his success—was his unflagging energy and the zest
with which he pursued any undertaking once begun.

Through his secretary and friend, Einhard, who knew him well, we see Charles as a 'tall, well-built man with large piercing eyes. Like many great men, he had a big nose. At the end of his life his hair was white, but abundant. His manner was impressive though affable, and held both authority and dignity.'

Charles kept his physical vigour until practically the end of his long life. He excelled as an athlete, and enjoyed hunting, swimming and bathing in the hot springs near his palace at Aachen. Although a barbarian and warrior, he had a keen intelligence and grew to revere learning. He attended the lectures in grammar of Peter of Pisa, a famous teacher brought to his court from Lombardy. For other subjects the Northumbrian Alcuin was his tutor. But the art of writing Charles only partially mastered, in spite of assiduous practice during his many wakeful hours (for the king was a poor sleeper). Unlike his sons, daughters and courtiers, he cared nothing for finery, although his dress was always suited to the occasion. On festal days his gold, bejewelled diadem was donned, as well as gilded boots, and a garment of cloth of gold surmounted by a golden cloak. But on other days his dress differed little from that of ordinary people, his favourite garb being a jerkin of otter skins or, for wet weather, one of fleece. As a rule, the national dress of upper-class Franks was rich and colourful. Charles' daughters, noted for their beauty, always wore magnificent costumes. His nobles also habitually appeared in gilded and laced boots, richly embroidered trousers of fine linen, bound below the knees with scarlet cross-garters. Embroidered linen shirts and a cloak of white or blue, cut in two squares, fastened at the shoulders and looped up at the sides, but ankle-length before and behind, completed their costume.

One of Einhard's anecdotes reveals Charles' common

sense regarding dress and also his somewhat mischievous humour. He had attended Mass one cold,
rainy day plainly attired and wearing a sheepskin.
His courtiers had just returned from Pavia, where they
had attended a fair to which the Venetians had
'carried all the wealth of the east from their territories
beyond the sea'. Having bought lavishly of these
wares they attended Mass

strutting in robes made of pheasant skins and silk; or
of the necks, backs and tails of peacocks in their first
plumage. Some were decorated with purple and
lemon coloured ribbons; some were draped round
with blankets and some in ermine robes.

The king, with a malicious twinkle, suddenly said,
'Let us go hunting . . . in the very clothes we are
wearing at this moment.' The nobles had to obey.
They scoured the thickets, were torn by branches of
trees, thorns and briars; they were drenched with
rain and defiled by the blood of wild beasts. In this
plight they returned home.

Then the most crafty Charles ordered, 'Let no-one
take off his dress of skins before he goes to bed; they
will dry better upon our bodies.'

Next day, Charles said to his chamberlain 'Give
my sheepskin a rub and bring it to me.' It came quite
white and perfectly sound. Then, when his bed-
raggled courtiers appeared, the king said 'Most
foolish of mortals! Which of these dresses is the most
valuable and useful—mine, bought for a piece of
silver, or yours, bought for pounds?'

Their eyes sank to the ground, for they could not
bear his most terrible censure.

The Chamberlain referred to in this anecdote was
but one of an army of officials through whom Charles'
palaces and household were governed. As well as being

Custodian of the Treasury, the Chamberlain also had charge of the king's wardrobe. The Count of the Palace, corresponding in some ways to the old Mayor of the Palace, but without his powers, was primarily an officer of justice who presided over the palace court when Charles was unable to do so. He also acted as ambassador, general, and in other official capacities. The Quartermaster's duties were to arrange lodgings for Charles and his retinue when they were travelling, and to assign rooms

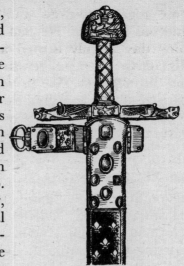

4   The hilt of Charlemagne's sword

to visitors in the palace when the court was in residence. The royal table was in the charge of the Seneschal, the Constable was Master of Horse, and for the Hunt there were four Masters. A hundred or more lesser officials included a Chief Door-keeper, a Chief Butler who was in charge of the cellars, and a Chief Falconer.

The greater part of Charles' life, however, was not spent in palaces, but as a warrior, and, to appreciate his achievements, and the great changes which he, his father Pepin and grandfather Charles Martel brought about, we must look at Europe when Charlemagne first became King of the Franks. In Spain, the Arabs were in possession. It was Charles Martel who had stopped their northward advance by defeating them near Poitiers in 732. Had he not been victorious, there was nothing to hinder the Moslems from marching to the Rhine. Pepin, Charlemagne's father, had dealt the

Arabs who remained north of the Pyrenees another
blow in a battle in the south of Aquitaine, and Charles
himself established a Spanish march south of the
Pyrenees, thus beginning the movement which was
eventually to drive the Moors from Spain. Nevertheless, Charles' army suffered a defeat—through
treachery it was said—at Roncesvalles, at the hands of
the Basques. From the legendary tales woven around
this battle evolved the *Song of Roland*, about a Breton
count of that name—a close friend of Charlemagne's—
who was killed at Roncesvalles. This poetic romance
set on fire the imagination of the later Middle Ages. At
Hastings in 1066, Taillefer the Jongleur went before the
Norman army, flinging his sword in the air and singing
stirring stanzas from the poem. By the twelfth century
the horn of Roland and the sword of Charlemagne had
become treasured relics—objects of the deepest venera-
tion to countless hosts of pilgrims.

Charlemagne's greatest struggle was against the
Saxons. They were pagans whose religion included
bloodthirsty rites. Together with the Frisians—a tribe
of farmers, traders and seamen—they lived across the
Rhine to the north and east of Francia. Charlemagne,
inspired by the Church, regarded his campaigns not
merely as wars of conquest but also as crusades. His aim
was to unify his dominions, to safeguard his frontiers
and to extirpate paganism as a step towards establishing
a great empire bound together by the Christian faith.
For this reason he destroyed Irminsul, the symbol of
the power of the Saxon gods, for it was this sacred trunk

5   The horn traditionally connected with Roland

which, they believed, upheld the vault of heaven. But
Charlemagne's sacri-
legious act, and the mass
baptisms they were
forced to undergo, the
Saxons never forgave.
As a result life among
them and among the
Frankish lands on their
borders was one of al-
most constant unrest
and bloodshed. For no
sooner was Charle-

6   Carolingian soldiers

magne removed to some distance than the Saxons
revolted. Then the monasteries and churches, trading
settlements and villages of the Franks went up in flames
of vengeance. Nevertheless, in spite of setbacks, Charlemagne, by the end of his long life, had subjugated
Lombardy and Saxony, restored and strengthened
Frankish authority in Bavaria and southern Gaul and
checked the Avars of the Middle Danube, as well as
adding much of Italy and the Spanish march to his
dominions.

To accomplish all this he had needed men and
soldiers on whom he could rely. He therefore exacted
an oath of allegiance from his subjects. Loyalty to an
oath was accounted one of the highest virtues among
barbarians. After revolts against him in 786 and in 792,
Charlemagne ordered that all men must renew their
oath of fealty or fidelity before one of the king's representatives. In every large town throughout the Frankish
domains, a stream of men attended the nearest church
and there publicly took an oath over the bones of a
saint. The words of an oath of fidelity taken after
Charlemagne had been made emperor have come down
to us:

I promise that, from this day forward, I will be the most faithful man of the most pious Emperor, my lord Charles, son of King Pepin and Queen Bertha; and I will be so in all sincerity, without deceit or ill-intention, for the honour of his kingship, as by right a man ought to behave towards his lord and master. May God and the saints, whose relics lie here before me, grant me their help; for to this end I shall devote and consecrate myself with all the intelligence that God has given me, for the remainder of my life.

An inner circle of men took an even more binding oath—that of vassalage. Vassalage grew to mean something more than mere allegiance. When, during the Crusades, Turpin the Archbishop hacked the Moslem chief rib from rib, the Christians shouted their triumph aloud calling 'He hath shown great vassalage'. So, in the *Song of Roland*:

> *Blancandrius was a pagan very wise,*
> *In vassalage he was a gallant knight,*
> *First in prowess he stood his lord beside.*

A vassal was usually rewarded for his services by royal gifts of land, so that in this way a great class of landed magnates grew up. Here we can see signs of that special form of organisation which was later to dominate feudal society. Wealth and authority were synonymous with ownership of land. On his manorial estate the lord, who was sometimes an abbot, stood at the head of a descending hierarchy of tenants. In a period when wars and famine were incessant, service, in exchange for protection, became the keynote of society. At the head was the king, who held two assemblies yearly, attended by his nobles and higher clergy. If a campaign were planned, all who owed military service were ordered to come to the gathering with their quota of the war host fully equipped and with all necessary supplies.

Charles' letter to Abbot Fulrad shows us an ecclesiastical magnate's armed train *en route* to the Mayfield, the name given to the spring assembly. He was ordered to come,

> so prepared with your men that you may be able to go thence well equipped in any direction which our command shall order, that is with arms and accoutrements and other provisions for war in the way of food and clothing. Each horseman is expected to have a shield, lance, sword, dagger, bow, quiver with arrows, and in your carts shall be . . . axes, planes, augers, boards, spades, iron shovels and other utensils which are necessary in any army. In the wagons shall be supplies for three months, together with arms and clothing for six months.

The duty of serving in the army or of contributing to its manpower and support was a universal obligation. Failure to do so involved the payment of sixty *solidi*, a fine so large as to make military service practically compulsory. One of Charles' capitularies or decrees dealt specifically with military obligations.

> Every free man who has four *mansi* (a *mansus* was about 135 acres), or who holds them as a benefice from anyone, shall equip himself and go to the army either with his lord or his count.
>
> He who has three *mansi* shall be joined to a man who has one *mansus*, and shall aid him so that he shall serve for both. . . .
>
> Four owners of one *mansus* shall each aid one of their number who shall go alone to the army.

But no aspect of government escaped Charles' attention and his capitularies deal with matters ranging from the rule of monasteries and the extradition of robbers from sanctuaries, to the protection of travellers, the prevention of serfs dying of starvation, and the education of female orphans by honourable matrons under the supervision of the clergy; for these, and a hundred other concerns, whether ecclesiastical, political, social, or judicial, Charles drew up regulations.

But the capitularies known as *De Villis*—directions to the stewards who managed the royal estates or 'vills' —are among the most detailed and stringent of any. Not an egg, a nail or a plank was to be omitted from the accounts which the king's managers had to render every Christmas. During the Carolingian period each estate or 'fisc' was divided into seigniorial and tributary lands. The former, known under the later manorial system as demesne lands, were under the direct control of the king, lord or abbot (if the estate were monastic).

Royal vills were numerous. Everything on them was of the finest quality whether they were horses, cattle, fruit, vegetables, flowers or ornamental birds like peacocks, for Charles had decreed that: 'Our vills, which we have founded for our own use, should wholly minister to our wants, not to those of others.'

The greatest care must be taken that whatever is prepared by hand—bacon, smoked meat, sausage, partially salted meat, wine, vinegar, mulberry wine, cooked wine, mustard, cheese, butter, malt, beer, mead, honey, wax, flour, all should be prepared with the greatest cleanliness. . . .

In each of our estates the chambers shall be provided with counterpanes, cushions, pillows, bedclothes, coverings for tables and benches.

Each estate was practically self-supporting, for every steward was to have in his district:

7   The Four Evangelists writing their Gospels in an outdoor scriptorium
An illumination from a manuscript of the eighth century

8 Peasants tilling the soil
From an early fourteenth-century English Psalter

9 Charlemagne presents a model of the Cathedral of Aix-la-Chapelle to
the Virgin
A detail from the shrine of Charlemagne at Aix-la-Chapelle

blacksmiths, a goldsmith, a silversmith, shoemakers, turners, carpenters, sword-makers, fishermen, foilers, soap-makers, men who know how to make beer . . . or other kind of liquor good to drink, bakers to make pastry for our table, net-makers to make nets for hunting, fishing and fowling, and other sorts of workmen too numerous to be designated.

Strict orders were also given that the dwellings of the women workers on the estate should have strong shutters, bolts and bars. The houses were to have cellars and stoves, so that the women could do their work properly. Plenty of raw materials must be provided by the steward: 'linen, wool, woad, vermilion, madder, wool-combs, teazels, soap, grease, and all necessary vessels'.

The estates of the Abbey of St Germain des Prés, near Paris, were run on similar lines. In the early ninth century there were only 25 slaves out of 278 householders on two of the abbot's fiscs. Four centuries later there were no slaves, but all except a few of the villagers had become serfs. Under Charlemagne the workers were mostly free, but services, money payments and rents in kind, due to the lord, varied according to the status of individuals.

One of the abbot's tenants was called Frambert. He lived in a small wooden house in a group of similar dwellings. During certain weeks of the year he and other tenants had to do a fixed amount of ploughing on the abbot's seigniorial lands. In addition the steward could call on him during busy weeks for extra labour. These types of service later became known as week and boon work. Frambert and his fellows performed other tasks for the abbot, such as felling trees, sawing logs or mending byres and fences. In addition Frambert had to pay in kind for certain privileges, a load of logs to the

abbey in return for gathering firewood in the woods, a
hogshead of wine made by Frambert's wife for the
right to pasture pigs in the same woods. Every tenant
of the king had to pay an army due, and he in turn
collected a share of it from his sub-tenants. Frambert's
contribution might be two shillings of silver or its
equivalent—perhaps an ox, or two sheep. This was in
addition to the direct military service which was also
demanded from him. Add to this extra contributions of
corn, wine, oil, chickens or eggs which had to be
supplied to the monastery by Frambert, until it seems
surprising that he ever had time or energy to cultivate
his own small farm or tend his own vines.

Frambert's wife was as hard-working as he. For her
there were children to tend, hens to feed, eggs to gather,
swine to be herded, vines to be dressed, and all the spinning, weaving, dyeing and making of cloth for tunics,
cloaks and hoods for the menfolk, and for herself and
her daughters the long, girdled robes that could be
hitched up when working. Yet even peasants had their
highdays and holidays. It was through the Church that
these were obtained and Charlemagne willingly made
a law, confirmed by his son in 827, to enforce the
Sabbath as a day of rest.

We ordain according to the law of God . . . that no
servile works shall be done on Sundays . . . tending
vines, ploughing fields, reaping corn and mowing,
working in quarries or building houses; nor shall
any man work in the garden, come to the lawcourts,
or follow the chase. But it is lawful on Sunday to
carry for the army, carry food, or carry (if need be)
the body of the lord to the grave.
Item, women shall do no textile work, nor cut out
clothes, nor stitch them with the needle, nor card
wool, nor beat hemp, nor wash clothes in public,

nor shear sheep; so that
they may rest on the
Lord's Day. But let
them come together
from all sides to Mass
in church.

Yet sometimes, on
saints' days, Frambert
and his friends brought
down upon themselves

10   Peasant harvesters

the censure of the Church. For they loved to dance and
sing on holy days, and these gaieties were often accompanied by immorality and sacrilege; for folksongs were
ribald and sometimes profane—a legacy from pagan
days. Dances, too, were not only performed in the
churchyard but in the church itself, even when services
were in progress. In one diocese a preacher had
forbidden the holding of dances in churches on saints'
days and festivals. But, in one parish,

> certain young folk were wont to come and ride upon
> a wooden horse and to dance masked and disguised
> in the church. One young man refused to give up the
> sport. When this aforesaid youth pranced upon his
> wooden horse into the church while the congregation
> were keeping vigils in peace and prayer, then, on the
> very threshold of the sanctuary a fire caught him by
> the feet and utterly consumed him, horse and man.

Mere dancing was not by any means the worst type
of transgression, for in many districts bloodthirsty
pagan rites were still practised, especially in those
which, like Saxony, had been recently conquered and
the population forced into baptism at the sword's
point. Everywhere, priests complained, 'all lures of
the devil' were ingrained in country folk. Yet Frambert
and his like could indulge in more harmless amuse-

11   A dancer and entertainer

ments. The alehouse was popular, especially when a wandering minstrel was present to sing profane songs and ballads about the warlike deeds of Frankish heroes. (Charlemagne himself delighted in such epics and had the barbarous and ancient lays written down so that he could commit them to memory at his leisure.)

But one month in the year was anticipated with especial pleasure by Frambert and indeed by all who lived within walking distance of Paris. This was the time of the great annual fair of St Denis which went on outside the city gates for the whole of October, 'to allow merchants from Italy, Spain, Provence and other countries to attend it'.

From Charlemagne's injunction to his stewards to prevent his 'workpeople from running about to markets and fairs', we know that tenants such as Frambert sometimes managed to evade their overseer and to escape with their wives and children to Paris, where they could spend some of their hard-earned silver pence on the delights of St Denis (*25*).

They would gape at the stalls displaying Venetian wares, at the cloaks of peacocks' feathers, at the rich silks and embossed leather. The children would stare, engrossed, at the display of pet monkeys or clamour for the rich sweetmeats made into shapes of pigs and cats. But most of all the peasants would goggle at the conjurer who could swallow fire or a sword and laugh uproariously at the antics of tumblers and jugglers or at a shabby bear dancing miserably at his master's bidding. Then, the day at an end, Frambert and his friends would trudge home with their families to begin again the gruelling daily round the following day. For, as one early writer asks of a poor ploughman, 'Is not your work very hard?' 'Indeed,' he answered, 'indeed, it is very hard.' With which, no doubt, all medieval Framberts would have agreed.

But not only land-workers had cause to complain of the hardness of their lot in Charles' kingdoms. For the king, besides turning his relentless vigour to the extermination of paganism outside his borders, waged an equally unflagging war against ignorance within them—to the dismay, no doubt, of many clerics and monks, ill-educated and often illiterate as they were.

> For it is expedient [the king wrote in a famous letter to Abbot Baugulf] that the bishoprics and monasteries entrusted by the favour of Christ to our government, in addition to the rule of monastic life, ought to be zealous also in the culture of letters. . . .
>
> Yet in recent years, when letters have been written to us from various monasteries to inform us that the brethren who dwelt there were offering on our behalf holy prayers, we noted in most of these letters, correct thoughts, but uncouth expressions; for what pious devotion dictated faithfully to the mind, the tongue, uneducated on account of neglect of study, was not able to express without error. . . .
>
> Therefore, we exhort you not to neglect the study of letters. . . . Such men are to be chosen for this work as have both the will and ability to learn and a desire to instruct others. And may this be done with a zeal as great as that which we command it.

During the 780s Charlemagne had brought to his court many scholars, who combined learning with a desire to instruct others. By their help he instituted a school in his palace where his own sons and other youths were taught. About 782 Paul the Deacon and his Italian colleagues took charge of this, among them Paulinus of Aquileia, a theologian, and Peter of Pisa, a grammarian. But from A.D. 782 to 796 Alcuin, a Northumbrian—a skilled teacher and writer from York in England—was the school's leading spirit.

Alcuin's method of teaching was mainly through dialogue. In one of these the young Prince Pippin asks questions which Alcuin answers:

Pippin: What is life?
Alcuin: The joy of the blessed, the sorrow of sinners, the expectation of death.
Pippin: What is death?
Alcuin: An unavoidable occurrence, an uncertain journey, the tears of the living, the confirmation of the testament, the thief of man.

During the Middle Ages the guessing of riddles was used both as a form of education for sharpening the wits, and as a source of entertainment. In the following, Alcuin sets a problem for Pippin:

Alcuin: Since thou art a youth of good abilities and natural gifts, I will put before thee some riddles.
  I have seen the dead create the living and the dead consumed by the breath of the living.
Pippin: From the rubbing together of sticks, fire is born which consumes them.

Dialogues in which Charles himself took part were usually of a more profound nature:

Charles: Expound the nature of justice.
Alcuin: Justice is a state of mind which assigns to

each thing its proper worth. In it the cult
of the divine, the rights of mankind, and the
equitable state of the whole life are preserved.

Charles: Unfold its parts also.

This Alcuin proceeds to do.

In many Carolingian schools it became customary
for pupils to specialise either as readers, singers or copy-
ists of manuscripts. As a result, certain schools became
famous either for their music or for the beauty of the
books they produced. That of Metz excelled in the
former, those of Tours, Fleury and Lyons in the latter
art. Although there was no comprehensive system of
elementary education in Charles' realms, yet individual
bishops, stimulated by the emperor's zeal, arranged
for the establishment of schools in every village of their
dioceses. There, taught by the local priest, any Christian father might send his children, without payment,
to learn to read and write. After Charles' death, during
the terrible years when his empire fell apart, the lamps
of education flickered and grew dim. Yet in the
cathedral and monastic schools they were never
completely extinguished. The love of books fostered by
Charles also lingered on. In every monastery of any
pretensions some provision remained for the copying of
manuscripts. Under Charles, in the larger monasteries,
so many scribes were employed that their *scriptoria,* or
writing rooms, were able to supply not only their own
libraries, but, from their surplus, those for other
monasteries as well. Library lists and manuscripts
which have survived prove that Carolingian collections
included a surprisingly large number of books, sacred
and pagan.

In one of his poems Alcuin included a brief summary of the contents of the cathedral library at York.

Among them were not only many works of the early
Church Fathers and poems by Christian writers, but
also those of pagan authors: the poetic works of Virgil,
Statius and Lucan, with some of the prose writings of
Cicero, the elder Pliny, Aristotle and Pompeius
Maurus, an African who wrote a commentary on
Donatus' grammar books in the sixth century.

In France, Corbie, Tours and Lyons could boast of
well-stocked libraries in the ninth century. Many
Corbie manuscripts later went to St Germain and are
owned today by the National Library of Paris. The
cathedral library of Lyons also retains many of its
early manuscripts.

During the eighth and ninth centuries, the libraries
in what are now Germany and Switzerland developed.
From the *scriptoria* of Cologne and Mainz came manuscripts which survive today. At Wurzburg, also, many
books made or collected by the early monks can still be
seen. The surviving catalogue of the famous library of
Lorsch in Hesse names nearly 600 works, both sacred
and classical, owned by that library. These included
treatises on grammar, rhetoric and metrics which were
used in the monastic school.

Some idea of the cost, difficulties and labour involved
in the production of these hand-written and illuminated books can be guessed from the note of Winitharius,
a monk of St Gall, in Switzerland. He personally
inscribed six manuscripts, wholly or in part, and writes
when finishing one of his books:

Here ends the book which Winitharius, a sinner and
a priest undeservedly ordained, wrote. With God's
help he brought it to completion by the work of
his own hands; there is not here a single leaf which
he has not obtained by his own efforts, either by
purchase or by begging for it, neither is there in

this book one apex or iota which his hand did not trace.

Produced at such a cost, manuscripts were precious possessions, and we find written into them exhortations to treat them with care, and sometimes curses upon would-be thieves. A ninth-century copy of Juvenal carries an inscription bidding the fires of Hell consume anyone who dared to steal it.

Another scribe, more restrainedly, begs his reader to 'turn the pages gently, wash your hands, hold the book so, and lay something between it and your dress'. It is to the dedication of these monks and scholars of the so-called 'Dark Ages' that we owe the preservation of so many ancient masterpieces which would otherwise have entirely perished.

Other arts also were encouraged and developed during Charles' reign, especially that of architecture. Vast palaces were built at Nimeguen, Ingelheim and Aachen, but it was to the building of churches that Charles devoted his zeal, his money and his gifts. The finest was the basilica of St Mary the Virgin at Aachen. Massive in style, perfect in proportions, adorned with choicest columns, marbles and mosaics from Ravenna, it was revealed as the most beautiful building of western Christendom. Gold and silver were used for its splendid candelabra, shining brass for its many doors and railings, solid gold for the apple on the roof.

Parts of Charles' building still remain in the present cathedral. An octagon in the style of S. Vitale at Ravenna, 50 feet in diameter, surrounded by a 16-sided gallery terminating in a cupola, it can still claim to be one of the most remarkable monuments of early Christian architecture. The gates of the archways and of the upper gallery, and the marble and granite columns date back to Charlemagne's time. Here also is

12   Reconstruction of Charlemagne's palace at Aachen

the emperor's stone throne which, excavated by
Otto III, Emperor of Germany (983–1002), symbolised for the kings of western Europe the idea of
empire and royal greatness. Charlemagne's early
basilica was connected by a portico with the royal
palace, above which stood an equestrian statue of
Theodoric brought from Ravenna. In what is regarded
as an authentic drawing of Charles in an early manuscript we see him in his imperial crown and robes
holding a model of the basilica and towers of St Mary,
with the bronze eagle—wings outspread—hovering
over the adjoining palace.

The church of St Riquier was also built under
Charlemagne's patronage. On this he and his family
and the great magnates bestowed a fabulous wealth of
gold and silver frontals for the altars, gold, silver and
bejewelled patens, chalices and sacred vessels, reli-
quary crosses and several hundred exquisite embroi-

dered vestments. Both palaces and churches were lavishly decorated with wall-paintings, stuccoes and terracotta, with bronze pillars and balustrades, all of a high order of artistic excellence.

Along with this flowering of architectural decoration went the development of manuscript illustration. New artists, some of them refugees from the Byzantine east, brought fresh ideas to the court at Aachen. One of the Gospel Books which they copied and illuminated is still at Aachen and the page on which the four evangelists, attended by their symbols, are shown composing their gospels, in a landscape of lapis rocks and stark trees against a sunset sky, is an exquisite work of art (7).

But the hope of further development in art and civilisation, and in the firm establishment of a Christian Empire was cut short, not only by Charlemagne's death but also by renewed attacks against western Europe by Saracen corsairs in the south, Norse pirates in the north, and the dreaded Magyar horsemen to the east. For another century and a half, European Christian civilisation had to fight for its very existence.

2

LORDS AND VASSALS

SOME 50 years after Charlemagne's death, his empire was, in 870, divided into three realms by the Treaty of Mersen. From these, the Kingdom of the East Franks, that of the West Franks and the kingdom of Italy, powerful modern states were later to develop (map, Fig. 2). But for centuries, no ruler was able to establish a central government strong enough to resist the new barbarian attacks or control the internecine strife of great landowners. In fact it was these—counts, margraves, bishops and other magnates—who from strongly fortified castles protected their own districts or waged war against a neighbouring landowner. In these activities they had private armies composed of their numerous vassals who were at their beck and call.

The fourteenth-century illustration (*13*) represents one of these vassals or feudal tenants with five arms, standing in a cornfield. Two of his hands, folded together are clasped in those of his seated overlord. One hand, pointing to himself, indicates that he is the lord's 'man'. With his two remaining hands he points to the cornfield, which represents his 'fief', or grant of land for which he is performing the rite of homage in the presence of the lord's court. The word 'homage' from the French word *homme* means the ceremony by which one man declares that he has become the 'man' of another. This ceremony was one of the most important rites performed during the period when western Europe was organised under feudalism. The origin of this can be traced partly to late Roman and partly to Germanic practices, at a time when men placed

13 Symbolization of the rite of homage

themselves under the protection of a man stronger and wealthier than themselves. In the eighth century we find such a man, entirely without resources addressing a certain 'magnificent lord'.

Inasmuch as it is known to all and sundry that I lack the wherewithal to feed and clothe myself, I have asked of your pity, and your goodwill has granted to me permission to deliver and commend myself into your authority and protection . . . in return you have undertaken to aid and sustain me in food and clothing, while I have undertaken to serve you and deserve well of you as far as lies in my power. And for as long as I shall live, I am bound to serve you and respect you as a free man ought, and during my lifetime I have not the right to withdraw from your authority and protection, but must, on the contrary, for the remainder of my days remain under it.

And in virtue of this action, if one of us wishes to alter the terms of the agreement, he can do so after paying a fine of ten solidi to the other. But the agreement itself shall remain in force. Whence it has seemed good to us that we should both draw up and confirm two documents of the same tenor, and this they have done.

Obligations resembling this were entered into at a much earlier date than the eighth century, but it was

between the tenth and thirteenth centuries that the
practice of commendation and other feudal institutions
reached their fullest development. Even so, they varied
widely in different parts of Europe, and farms and
holdings, free from all rents and obligations, were
found scattered among the feudal estates. In spite of
wide divergences in feudal custom it is possible to give a
general picture of the relationship that existed between
lords and their vassals and of the manner in which they
held their fiefs, though it must never be forgotten that
feudalism developed in different districts and countries
along individual lines.

During the break-up of the Carolingian empire, and
the period of devastation under Norse, Hungarian and
Saracen raids, long-distance trade was destroyed and
what gold remained in western Christendom drained
away to Moslem or Byzantine coffers. Land, not money,
then became the chief form of wealth. Those who
owned land, owned the possibility of building up
military and political power, for on land men could
grow food, and men could be settled to serve and to
fight for their overlords. During these disturbed
centuries free men again commended themselves in
great numbers of their own free will, to the power,
service and protection of a strong lord. In 1127, a
contemporary has described how the vassals of the
murdered Count of Flanders hastened to put themselves
under the protection of his successor, Count William
Clito:

First they did homage in the following manner. The
count demanded of the future vassal if he wished
without reserve to be his man, and he replied, 'I wish
it'. Then, with his hands clasped and enclosed between
those of the count this alliance was sealed by a kiss.
Secondly, he who had done homage engaged his

faith to the count in the following words: 'I promise by my faith, that from this time forward I will be faithful to Count William and will maintain towards him my homage entirely against every man, in good faith and without any deception.' Thirdly, all this was sworn on the relics of saints.

The kiss was not an essential part of the act of homage, but it emphasised that both master and man were on the same level of friendship, that there was nothing derogatory in vassalage. In Germany, where the chiefs of great families disliked submitting to what they regarded as servile bonds, or to admitting that their vassals were their equals in friendship, the kiss of equality as between freemen and comrades was omitted.

A vassal had to perform certain services for his lord; in the case of superior tenants this was usually military in character. In the early days retainers lived in their leader's stronghold which was at first of the motte and bailey type. A visit of the Bishop of Térouenne to the motte of Merchem near Dixmüde is described in 1130 by a contemporary:

Near the churchyard was an exceeding high fortification built according to the fashion of that country by the lord of the manor many years ago. For it was customary for the rich men and nobles of those parts —because their chief occupation is the carrying on of feuds and slaughters, in order that they may have the greater power for either conquering their equals or keeping down their inferiors—to heap up a mound of earth as high as they were able and to dig round it a broad, open and deep ditch, and to girdle the whole upper edge of the mound with a strong wall of hewn logs, stoutly fixed together. Within was constructed a house, or rather a citadel, commanding the whole, so that the gate of entry could only be approached by a bridge, which, springing from the outer lip of the ditch, rested on the mound near the entrance.

The bishop, having completed his ceremonies in the church, returned to the citadel, to change his vestments. On the bridge the townsfolk had gathered to see him pass. The additional weight of the bishop and his retinue was more than the structure could bear. With a rending crash it collapsed, throwing its occupants, both lay and clerical, 35 feet into the ditch below.

Life in such a military tower must have been hard and rough. Lambert of Ardres gives a contemporary account of the domestic arrangements in a motte built in his native town in 1117:

Arnold of Ardres built on the motte there a wooden house, excelling all the houses of Flanders in that period both in material and carpenters' work. The ground floor contained great boxes, casks, and other domestic utensils. Above were dwelling rooms and the great chamber in which the lord and his wife slept. In the inner part of the great chamber was a certain private room, where at early dawn, or in the evening, or during sickness or time of blood-letting, or for warming the maids and weaned children, they used to have a fire. Adjoining this was a private dormitory for waiting maids and children. In the upper storey were garret rooms, in which on one side the sons slept, on the other, the daughters. Here also, watchmen appointed to keep guard slept at one time or another. There were stairs and passages from house to kitchen—an adjoining building of two floors. Stairs led from house to loggia where they used to sit in conversation, and from the loggia to the oratory.

In the bailey were stables and rooms for the garrison with kitchens and workshops near by.

Fulk de Nerra, Count of Anjou (987–1040) who consolidated the greatness of his line begun by his forbears, was a typical feudal lord—powerful and ruthless. He was a pioneer in the building of stone fortresses. The keep he erected at Langeais (994–5) still, after almost a thousand years, symbolises all Fulk's ferocity and will to hold what he had gained. Throughout the following four centuries, castles were erected on ever-more elaborate plans, like that of Château Gaillard built in Normandy by Richard II of England in the thirteenth century. This had three wards or courtyards—an outer, middle and inner. All were surrounded by immensely strong walls with towers at intervals and also by an outer moat. The inner ward at Château Gaillard had its own moat and was moreover built on a high rocky promontory so that the donjon or keep within it was almost impregnable. This fortified tower provided a final refuge for the defenders if the enemy had succeeded in taking the wards. Doorways to castles had their own defensive towers, a drawbridge that could be raised or lowered at will, and a portcullis—a movable trellised screen of beams and

14   The ruined keep of Langeais

iron—which could be let down from above. Such
fortresses, when not royal or held by a supporter of the
king, could be a threat to the ruler's authority; they
were also bases from which magnates could wage
internecine war against each other.

In the centuries of disorder it was essential for an
ambitious man who wished to hold or gain power to
have a strong force of knights and fighting men. To
attract and reward followers, kings, princes and lesser
magnates granted fiefs to their retainers. These were
usually landed estates varying in size from a few acres
to a thousand or more. They could be held directly
from the king, from an abbey or from a layman not
necessarily of superior rank, to his vassal. Tolls and
market dues, rights of minting and justice, the holding
of offices, such as that of a mayor, a receiver or a steward,
or those of carpenters and painters, could be granted as
fiefs. In the twelfth century even money payments were
made into fiefs. Then there were vassals who agreed to
serve their lord in war, wearing the long coat of mail
known as a hauberk—they held a 'fief de hauberk'.
Some had to serve as guards in the lord's castle; others
to give financial aid, while overlords often had rights of
marriage and wardship over their tenants' children;
indeed fiefs were granted on innumerable conditions of
service, many of which were irksome in the extreme.

Among lands held as fiefs by vassals were estates and
farms held by free men and completely free of service.
These 'allods', as they were called, were from time to
time surrendered for a variety of reasons by their
owners and received back as fiefs. In 1071, Robert the
Frisian usurped the county of Hainault, killing the
young Count Arnulf III during the struggle. Arnulf's
mother, the widowed Countess Richalda determined to
oust the usurper and put her younger son Baldwin in
his place. So she

sold her allods in Hainault to the Bishop of Liège.
With the purchase money she intended to hire
mercenaries to use against Robert. Bishop Theoduin
gladly received these great allods, which such an
honour made illustrious. He granted them back to
Richalda and Baldwin to be held as a liege fief from
him and he paid a very great sum for them.

When a fief was granted to a vassal, this also became
the occasion for a symbolic ceremony. The people of
the Middle Ages seldom thought in abstract terms.
Whatever act was performed, from the coronation of a
king to the freeing of a serf, it had to be accompanied
by a symbolic drama performed in public. In days
when written contracts were rare, this dramatisation
helped to impress the event on the memory of witnesses,
who might later be called on to testify as to when and
whether a baptism had taken place, a marriage solem-
nised, or whether certain claimants had indeed been
enfeoffed with specific fields.

Investiture followed the act of homage and the oath
of fealty. Only in northern Italy was a man invested
with his fief before he had taken the oath of fealty. A
twelfth-century poem describes an investiture by
Charlemagne:

Bérard of Montdidier before Charles has come.
At his feet he kneels his man to become.
The emperor kisses him, makes him to stand,
By giving him a white ensign he enfeoffs him in his land.

Sometimes a clod of earth, a bunch of corn or a banner
or lance was handed to the vassal; these symbolised that
he had been given seisin of his land. In the thirteenth
century, however, it became more common in France,
England and Flanders, for a lord to give his vassal a
charter on which it was stated that the acts of fealty,

15   Investiture by ensign

homage and investiture had been performed for a certain fief. Sometimes the vassal gave a document regarding the transactions to his lord. In 1228 one of these documents ran as follows: 'Messire J. d'Estenville has done homage to William, Bishop of Paris, for what he holds of him near Sainte-Croix, at Saint-Denis, and he undertakes to provide within 40 days a list in writing to the bishop of what these things are.'

Such feudal legalities between a man and his lord did not preclude a close personal relationship between them. Besides giving military service a vassal often served on his lord's council. On liturgical feast days he would be summoned to the castle and there be royally entertained. Many descriptions exist of these great ceremonial gatherings, of lords and ladies in velvet, silk and samite, of squires and maidens in embroidered garments. We hear the trumpeters (*16*) sound the call to dinner in the great hall where the feast will last for hours; we listen to minstrels and jongleurs singing their songs of battle and love:

> *Look on this rose, O Rose,*
> *And looking laugh on me,*
> *And in thy laughter's ring*
> *The nightingale shall sing.*
>
> *Take thou this rose, O Rose,*
> *Since Love's own flower it is,*
> *And by that rose,*
> *Thy lover captive is.*

Then follow tumblers, fools and jesters, and the presentation of gifts to the vassals, of horses, arms and vestments. Perhaps the next morning the lord would gather his councillors round him 'to render justice . . . give help to the oppressed'; then a discussion regarding estate management might follow, perhaps about the desirability of felling wood—or, more likely, there would be a lively discussion about some forthcoming campaign.

One of the major virtues of the Middle Ages was loyalty to one's lord; indeed the tie between vassal and lord was almost as strong as that of blood. Frederick Barbarossa decreed in Germany that an incendiary who had taken refuge in a castle must be delivered to justice unless he were the castle-owner's 'lord, his vassal or his kinsman'. The custom of sending children to be brought up in the lord's castle usually strengthened the bond of affection that bound them together. We have a vivid picture of the child Garnier in Charlemagne's household:

> *When the king goes to the forest, the child goes too.*
> *His bow he sometimes bears, his stirrup often holds.*
> *When after wildfowl runs the king, Garnier is close behind.*
> *The hawk or sharp-eyed falcon sits upon his wrist,*
> *And when to bed the king retires, Garnier attends him there,*
> *Singing sweet songs to him or old, heroic lays.*

The romance of *Galeran* pictures for us another young squire who, after two years, is dubbed a knight by the duke he had been serving. For the keystone of early feudalism was the heavily armed and mounted knight. Such was his importance that the Church early gave its blessing to the order of knighthood, and it was generally recognised that 'knights should be honoured above all other men, save priests'. As time went on the order developed into a military caste, although at first any knight had been able to dub another a knight. But as early as 1119, when the Order of Knights Templars was founded for service in the Holy Land, it was divided into knights who wore white mantles and surcoats with a red cross on them, and 'serjeants' whose white mantles were contrasted with brown. No strict rule seems to have existed at this time regarding necessary qualifications for entering the higher rank. But by 1250 it was essential not only to be a knight, but 'a knight's son, or the descendant of a knight on his father's side', before a man was admitted to the superior rank of the Knights Templars.

This attempt to exclude from the ranks of knighthood any not of knightly lineage was not confined to the Templars, neither was it successful. In the thirteenth century we are told an amusing story of three knights, who, wishing to enter some undertaking that needed a fourth knight, seized upon a passing peasant, thrust him on to his knees, and with a 'Be thou a knight' carried him off to do their will. This illegal action was punished by a heavy fine, for by this date only the king could admit to knighthood any man not of knightly lineage.

A special ceremony had inevitably developed with its appropriate symbolism for the dubbing of a new knight. During the eleventh century it had been sufficient for an older knight to hand the squire a sword and give him a heavy blow with the flat of his hand on face or neck. The new knight was then expected to leap on to his horse and, lance in hand, charge at a quintaine, or suit of armour hanging on a post, and otherwise show off his prowess as a horseman and potential warrior.

But by 1150, the Church had taken over and tried to canalise war into 'righteous' channels. The candidate for knighthood carried his sword to the priest, who laid it on the altar; prayers were then said over it. A thirteenth-century prayer shows the attempt made to confine the use of the sword to causes which were 'just and right':

> Most Holy Lord, Almighty Father . . . thou who has permitted on earth the use of the sword to suppress the malice of the wicked and defend justice; who for the protection of thy people hast thought fit to institute the order of chivalry . . . cause thy servant here before thee, by disposing his heart to goodness, never to use this sword or another, to injure anyone unjustly; but let him use it always to defend the Just and Right.

In later centuries the ceremony was elaborated. The candidate's hair was cut, which, like the tonsure of a monk, symbolised his devotion to God. He might be

16 Sounding the trumpets for a meal

bathed and put to bed to represent the purification and
the rest enjoyed by the righteous in Paradise. By
donning three robes, a white, then a red with a black
one over it, the candidate signified his entrance into a
state of purity, of willingness to die for God's cause and
his acceptance of death. Back in the castle, the new
knight would be ceremonially robed and armed.
Galeran, in the romance of that name, put on a
hauberk, shoes and helmet. Over this he wore a blue
cloak with his crest of the double eagle embroidered on
it. From the duke himself he received his right spur and
a magnificent eastern sword with golden hilt, its blade
shining and inscribed with letters. A famous knight
girded on the sword for Galeran, who, kneeling received
from the duke the accolade of knighthood with the
words: 'Knight, God grant you a life of honour, that
you may be a *prud'homme*, in thought, word and deed.'

The duchess then hung the shield with its device of
eagles round his neck, and all the company went to
Mass. After it, Galeran removed his armour and put on
robes of silk to attend a great feast. The following day
he tourneyed for the first time:

> Then Galeran goes with a train of 30 packhorses and
> 10 Spanish chargers to Metz. The streets, strewn with
> herbs are full of knights on horseback, of squires
> carrying presents to ladies, of young men airing their
> hawks. Coloured banners and shields hang out of the
> windows—the walls are gay with festal drapery. The
> market is full: venison, game, fish, wax, pepper and
> spice are displayed. Moneychangers shout their
> wares of jewels and plate; the mountebanks, with
> their lions, leopards and bears, the fiddlers and
> singers wander round, and over all, the church bells
> ring through the town, filling the air with gay and
> cheerful sounds, give the new knights spirit for the
> morrow's jousting.

17   Ceremonial robing and arming of a knight

Knights were often created before or after a conflict. Philip the Fair gave the accolade to a butcher for his gallantry during the battle of Mons-en-Pevèle, despite persistent attempts to exclude all but knightly candidates from the order of knighthood. It was even forbidden to peasants to carry the knightly weapons of the lance and sword. Yet a poet's lament of 1160—'Ah God! how badly is the good warrior rewarded who makes the son of a villein a knight!'—indicates that serfs were able to breach the fortifications of knightly privilege. But the usual medieval view was that servile workers existed for the sake of the two higher orders— the fighters and those who prayed, especially, as Ramon Lull points out, they were ordained to support the knightly warriors:

> It is seemly that men should plough and dig and work hard in order that the earth may yield the fruits from which the knight and his horse will live; and that the knight who rides and does a lord's work, should get his wealth from the things on which his men are to spend much toil and fatigue.

How had this class of serfs arisen in the first place? Some at least had given up their free status in exchange for protection; but, not being suitable to enter the ranks of fighting men, they had had to surrender their persons and sometimes their land (if they had any) in

exchange for food, clothing and a hut to live in. Such a
one was William, brother of Reginald, who in the
eleventh century surrendered himself to the monks of
Marmoutiers, near Tours—'for the love of God' it was
stated, but this was merely a pious figment:

> Be it known to all who come after us that a certain
> man in our service, William, brother of Reginald,
> born of free parents, being moved by the love of
> God . . . gave himself up as a serf to St Martin of
> Marmoutiers, and he gave not only himself but all his
> descendants, so that they should forever serve the
> abbot and monks of this place in a servile condition.
> And in order that this gift might be made more
> certain and apparent, he put the bell rope round his
> neck and placed four pennies from his own head on
> the altar of St Martin in recognition of serfdom, and
> so offered himself to almighty God. The following are
> witnesses who saw and heard what was done. . . .

William had bound not only himself but his descendants 'for ever' to serfdom. True, free men often had
to work as hard, owed as many dues and services, and
often lived under the same condition as serfs. Indeed
everyone owed services and obligations of some sort to
those below and above them. Even free knightly tenants
inherited obligations with their estates and could not
escape from them or di-
minish them except by sur-
rendering their land.
Monks and Crusaders used
the same symbolism as William to indicate they had
become serfs of God. The
Pope himself bore the title
'servant of the servants of
God'. Such service did not

18   Knighting on the battlefield

hold any stigma. But William's descendants inherited a position that was regarded with contempt.

Yet without the work done by serfs on the manorial estates the whole complicated fabric of medieval agriculture, on which monasticism and feudalism was built, would have collapsed. For, although there were allods and free farms, the great part of western Christendom was organised under the manorial system. The lord had his demesne lands, cultivated by the workers who lived on the estate, both serfs and free men. The produce of demesne lands belonged to the lord. The peasants owed the lord dues, often paid in kind. For instance, one serf gave his lord a bushel of wheat, 18 sheaves of oats, three hens and one cock each year and five eggs at Easter. In addition he had to work three days in every week for the lord except at Christmas, Easter and Whitsuntide, when he had a week free. But each worker held his land under different conditions according to the amount he had. There was also an obligation for the serf to use the lord's mill, wine-press, oven and sheepfold, and, of course, to pay a fee for doing so. His house and lands, also, were in danger of being devastated by civil war and his crops trampled by the lord's hunting parties, or raided by wild game. Even worse, his property was, in theory at least, liable to seizure by the lord. In addition, no serf could marry any but a bondwoman within his own manor, nor enter holy orders except by his lord's permission. He also had to pay a poll tax, symbolised by the four pennies which 'William, brother of Reginald' had had on his head. Yet hardest of all to bear was the stigma of being held in contempt by all free men. Nevertheless, his condition was better than that of a slave. He was not a chattel, he had defined rights, and, though bound to his lord 'from the crown of his head to the soles of his feet' as one owner put it, he was not in all districts bound to the soil.

But in the eleventh century the unprecedented
expansion that took place in Europe gave new opportunities to the serf to escape from his thraldom. New
methods of agriculture made it possible to develop the
waste lands of Christendom. An increase in population
made this imperative, while providing simultaneously
the labour to bring new lands into cultivation. The use
of a heavier plough with an iron coulter to cut deeply
into the soil, and the addition of a mouldboard which
made furrows, greatly increased the yield of crops;
while the invention of the shoulder collar and the
harnessing of draught animals one behind another
made it possible for them to pull heavier loads. These
improvements, along with the use of water power for
grinding corn, contributed to the freeing of labour at a
time when lords were everywhere crying out for
tenants to clear new lands. Favourable conditions of
tenure were offered for these and the lords of old
estates—unless they wished to see their peasants
desert them—had to extend new privileges and remove
the heaviest burdens from their workers.

We can watch a French family arriving to settle on
new land near Sarthe where the count was eager to
welcome colonists. Robert Grafard wanted to set up a
farm on land that lay well outside the walls of the new
ville, or town, that had been built. He was lucky in
having a wife and two stalwart sons to help him. Even

19   Water-mill with eel traps in the stream

had he been of servile status before, he would now be able to establish himself as a free man and even to bargain with the count as to what rents he would pay and what services he would perform. He might be able to get the lord to provide him with a pair of oxen for his plough, and, if lucky, obtain some plots of *ouches*— fertile land where wheat could be grown. But Robert's first task was to fell trees and to build a house in the clearing made. Next he planted a garden where peas, beans, flax and hemp could be grown. A meadow provided grassland while the right to cut wood in the count's forest gave him material for farm buildings, fences, barrel hoops and fuel; he also had the right to feed his pigs there.

Hundreds of new, independent farms, as well as new *villes* and burgs, sprang up at this time, where former serfs could settle as free men. Many stewards and estate officials of servile birth also took advantage of the disturbed times and shortage of labour to seize the lands and rents of their lord. Jan, the steward of the Abbey of Brabant did this. He retained rents and claimed abbey lands for his own. His son Macarius went further. After fortifying his house and arming his servants, he so threatened the abbot that in 1146 the terrified cleric was forced to give legal sanction to the depredations of father and son, his former serfs. In Germany and France it became common for cellarers, stewards, foresters and other manorial officials to seize land and money which they had formerly administered and to become landed men with serfs of their own.

A serf sometimes became free by manumission or buying his freedom. Primitive law required that a master on freeing a serf should—before witnesses— take him to the open door of his house and set him upon the open road. By these symbolic acts he became a free man.

Increase in the flow of trade brought money into the
peasants' coffers and affected the life of remote villages.
By the thirteenth century, commerce was in full swing
once more. Venice, like other ports, was exporting
grain, oil, timber, fruit, animals, and meat—all country
products, and everywhere merchants and their agents
were searching inaccessible regions for goods to export.
One day in June 1236, villagers in the remote mountain
village of Tessero near Trent, watched the arrival of a
wealthy merchant—Corrado of Ora—and his train.
They saw him dismount from his horse outside the
house of Otto Grasso, an Italian landowner. In the
cool tiled living-room other men of standing had
gathered to witness a transaction whereby, in return
for £200 Veronese, Corrado was to have delivered in
November to himself or his agent, 500 *modii* of cereals—
rye, grain, beans, pot-herbs, and millet—and this was
to be not a single arrangement but was to continue for
several years.

In the same way, Florentine traders went to Apulia
to buy up cheese, others to bargain for '20 timbers of fir
to be delivered on the bank of the Aviso River at the
head of the bridge, or beyond it'. These are only three

transactions from hun-
dreds of records. But be-
hind the bare facts we
can see traders moving
over a Europe surging
afresh with commercial
life, and behind them,
in remotest districts,
peasants on virgin and
fertile lands, ploughing,
sowing, mowing, reap-
ing, making cheeses,
boys pounding salt for

20   German packhorses

the curd, wives sheep-shearing, packing up the fleeces, other men felling and transporting trees, or hunting for fur and flesh. As a result a new Europe came into being. Magnificent churches and palaces, libraries, universities, hospitals, cities were raised with money freely flowing once again. And a part of that wealth, infinitesimal perhaps, but important, went to the peasant, to buy his freedom, to pay for his sons' education, his daughters' dowries, to unlock the door into a new life and status for the descendants of that William, brother of Reginald, who had put the bell rope round his neck two centuries before. Trade also made changes in the higher levels of society. Up to the twelfth century ownership of land on a large scale had been the prerogative of the nobility, but the great commercial magnates of Flanders and Italy now formed an urban patriciate which ousted the feudal nobles from power. They, however, aped the manners and life of the former magnates and with some of their wealth bought country estates.

One of the lesser Italian merchants, Francesco Datini (26), has left a mass of letters and accounts which throw considerable light on his activities. He, too, although he had inherited his wife's family estate, delighted in buying up parcels of land near his birthplace, Prato. On his main farm there were two labourers, a stable containing horses and donkeys, a shed and a tower with a dovecote. Datini built new houses for his labourers, which brought a protest from his friend, 'If you put them into houses fit for craftsmen they will die of heat'. Nevertheless this same friend showed a humane attitude to his workers. Writing to Datini he states:

I have kept Moco, my labourer, for many a year, though when his sons were old enough to be of use

God took them from him, so that I have always had him alone. And he is so solicitous at the plough, and such a fine vine-pruner, that I know not how to make a change. . . . But I have found a large family whom I wish to place on my farm. My cowardly or compassionate soul (I know not which) knows not how to say to Moco 'Look for another farm'. . . . Tell me therefore within eight or ten days, if you have aught for him.

Not all Italians thought so highly of their peasants. One warns a townsman landowner in the fourteenth century to visit his lands as seldom as possible, and never on feast days, when all the workers gathered on the threshing floor:

for then they are heated with wine and are armed and there is no reasoning with them. Each one thinks himself a king and wants to talk, for they spend all their week with no-one to talk to but their beasts. Go rather to their fields when they are working—thanks to the plough, hoe or spade, you will find them humble and meek.

More than two centuries earlier Orfredo the jurist wrote:

If a knight be alone with a rustic and even threaten him with putting out his eyes, the man replies not; but if rustics be together, they shout against him and would even pull him off his horse. When they are together they will do any evil thing, but when alone, they are naught but hens.

Continuous work—apart from saints' days—and servitude were far from being the worst conditions under which peasants lived. Famine, particularly before the twelfth century, was frequent, and one

21 At the Battle of Crécy English long-bowmen helped defeat the heavy
French cavalry and cross-bowmen

chronicler tells us that in a very bad year human flesh
was on sale in the market. During the fourteenth
century the peasants of France and Italy in particular
suffered from the scourge of war. In both countries
bands of mercenaries roamed the countryside preying
on the inhabitants. Sir John Hawkwood's 'White
Company' was one of the most famous of these. On
news of the approach of soldiers, peasants gathered
what they could of their own and their master's goods,
put some food and the young children into carts, and,
driving their livestock before them, took refuge in the
nearest walled town. Often, however, peasants were
surprised ploughing in the fields, while from farm or
village their wives and daughters were carried off and
the buildings burned. Datini's farm of Il Paco was
threatened by approaching troops in 1397. The
merchant wrote from Florence to his wife:

See to it, with Barzalone and Niccolo, that all things
in Il Paco are brought to Prato, and that nothing
remains there, not even pieces of iron, for all is in

danger. For this eve, the soldiers came within 12 miles from here. And also bring in the straw at Chiusure and put it wherever you think best, for if the beasts cannot have oats, they must do with straw.

Plague and disease were further evils with which the peasant, along with the rest of medieval society, had to contend. But the Black Death of the mid-fourteenth century, by causing a chronic shortage of labour, enabled surviving peasants to make better terms with their landlords. By then, too, lords and knights did not form such an important branch of the armed forces. They were being superseded by archers and footmen who, drawn from outside the magnate and knightly classes, proved more effective on the field than their superiors. Nevertheless lords and serfs were to continue throughout the Middle Ages and beyond; there were still serfs in both France and Prussia in the eighteenth century. But on the whole, the position of workers gradually improved. A medieval poet tersely expresses man's inborn love of freedom in *The Bruce*:

> *For Freedom is a noble thing.*
> *Who Freedom hath, hath great liking.*

3

TOWNSMEN AND TRADERS

ONE of the strongest forces which was later to be most powerful in the undermining of feudal privilege was the growth of trade and the consequent restoration of a flourishing urban life in western Europe. Long before the fall of Rome, both commerce and towns had been undergoing a process of decay. Wealthy patricians had retired to a self-sufficient existence in comfortable villas on their country estates, while disorganisation, depopulation and poverty worked havoc with the towns. In manor houses and farms in the countryside owned by great landowners, as well as in monasteries, civilisation and culture maintained a precarious existence, meantime the barbarian incursions completed the destruction of most centres of urban life.

By the end of the sixth century the various tribes had, for a time at least, settled down—the Franks and Burgundians in what later became France and the Rhineland, the Visigoths in Spain, the Vandals along the North African coast (22), and eventually the Lombards in North Italy. Here, some great towns had been kept alive and even prosperous by the continuation of Mediterranean trade. In northern Europe also, those towns which had become the centre of bishoprics managed to maintain a comparatively stable life. The bishop, as early as the time of Constantine (323–53), acting as a leading magistrate, administering justice and settling disputes, had, with assistant priests, con-

22   Vandal leaving his African villa

trolled his diocese through an organisation modelled
on that of imperial Rome. The Merovingian kings of
the Franks, although no lovers of towns, nevertheless,
after their conversion to Christianity, attended important religious ceremonies in the capitals of the
various dioceses. These, conducted with a pomp and
splendour vividly described by Gregory of Tours, drew
thousands into the towns and contributed to their
survival. The establishment of early monasteries
outside the walls of other towns also helped these to
continue to function. When their pious founders died,
Christians came on pilgrimage to their shrines. Towns
like Tours, Reims and Brioude became prosperous,
catering for the needs of the devout who came there to
seek help or healing from the relics of St Martin, St
Remy or St Julian.

In spite of disturbed times, some towns had managed
to carry on ancient industries. In Cologne, glass
continued to be manufactured by a colony of Syrians.
Indeed, it was largely owing to the enterprise of eastern
merchants and craftsmen that trade in western Europe
did not cease in these early centuries. In the interior
provinces of France and Germany Jews seem to have
had a monopoly of trade. On the occasion when King
Guntram entered Orléans, greetings in Syrian and

Hebrew almost drowned those of the Latin-speaking townsmen. During both Merovingian and Carolingian times it was mainly easterners who held the positions of *negotiatores*—agents officially appointed to buy goods for the king and his household. Solomon the Jew was one of King Dagobert's merchants, while Priscus, also a Jew, acted

23   A tenth-century Frankish cart

in the same capacity for King Chilperic. Many Syrians and Greeks were at the court of Charlemagne, and it was with their help that a corrected version of the Four Gospels was achieved. Under Louis the Pious—Charlemagne's son—official palace merchants enjoyed extensive credit. Many of these were Jews, and Bishop Agobard reproached the king for favouring them, saying that their concessions had been extorted by violence. Nevertheless they obtained many luxury goods for the king and his nobles—spices, silks and brocades from the East—and more humdrum commodities for use in court offices and workrooms— papyrus and indigo for dyeing, and oil. After the Moslem conquest of Africa, Spain and the Mediterranean islands, French trade by sea almost ceased and wax, butter, parchment, woad and vegetable dyes were substituted for their corresponding eastern products.

In Carolingian Lyons, Jews were numerous enough to own several synagogues, as well as houses and lands, run by slaves and well supplied with wine and other luxuries. In fact, they were so predominant in France that ordinances concerning trade were addressed to

'Jews and other merchants'. A Persian scholar of the
tenth century has pictured the Jews of the ninth for us:

> These merchants speak Arabic, Persian, Greek and
> Latin, Frankish, Spanish and Slavonic. They travel
> from the extreme West to the extreme East, by land
> and by sea. From the West they bring eunuchs, slave
> girls and boys, brocade, beaver-skins, marten and all
> kinds of furs and swords.

He describes them as sailing from the 'Frankish shore'
(southern Italy or France). They disembark at the Nile
Delta, in Syria, or in Constantinople. Then, 'loading
their merchandise on the backs of camels, they proceed
by land to the Red Sea or to the Persian Gulf where they
embark for their journey by sea to India or China.'

There were overland routes, also, from Spain through
North Africa to Damascus and on to Baghdad, Persia
and India. 'The route behind Rome' went through the
lands of the Slavs into modern Russia and so to China.
Jews followed them all, for where trade was, there was
the Jew also—in Prague, city of stone, where dark-
skinned southerners paid for goods in Arab coins, and
fur-clad Baltic traders paid in kind with bales of cloth
and furs; in the wooden houses of Itil on the Volga,
where the Khazars had been converted to Judaism and
Jewish merchants were always sure of a welcome; in
Samkarsh, the fortified settlement of the Jews on the
Sea of Azov; and in the East where they established
banking houses, so that their brethren in western
Europe were able, when money there was scarce, to
lend it to the kings of France, Germany and Italy.

By the seventh century European merchant adventurers were emerging. Samo of Senon, during Dagobert's reign, journeyed to Esclavonia (Bohemia) to sell
arms and buy slaves. The former transaction was
against the Frankish law, but that would not deter

Samo. Eventually, he succeeded so well with the barbarian Wends that he ended by becoming their king.

The Frisians, as a nation, were also intrepid traders.
They lived on the sea coast and islands to the north of
the Rhine estuary. Missionaries sometimes journeyed
on their ships, and in the ninth century St Anscarius
shared the discomforts and dangers of a trading journey
to Schleswig, then on to Birka, the centre of Swedish
trade in the Baltic; but the saint's object was to gather
in souls, not *solidi*. The Frisians also traded with
England, and, like the English, used the port of
Quentovic (near modern Étaples) for entry into
Europe. Rouen and Amiens were towns with which
they traded, and they regularly attended the Fair of
St Denis, near Paris, founded by Dagobert. Their ships
sailed down the Rhine taking wine and corn from
Alsace, receiving cloth and fish in exchange. Mainz
was probably their chief depot, as merchants gathered
from far afield to trade there. Scandinavians also were
explorers, traders and later raiders. They voyaged as
far as the Bosphorus in the East and to Greenland and
Vinland—now thought to be Scatari Island—off the
coast of Nova Scotia.

24   Scene at a cloth market

In the eighth and ninth centuries trade with Lombardy also revived. Salt was carried along the Po and the men of Cremona were prosperous enough to acquire their own boats; the rich monasteries of Lombardy also established cells at Pavia where they sold their surplus produce to merchants going to and fro, and also to the urban population. The merchants of Commachio near the mouth of the Po sailed by royal charter, loading salt, oil and also spices and silk—brought from the East by Byzantine merchants—on to their picturesque boats, with orange and brown sails painted with signs of the zodiac. These goods they carried into the interior cities of the Lombard plain.

But the most lucrative and also most bestial trade was that in slaves. Many of these were Slavs who had moved east across the Elbe to occupy lands vacated by Germanic peoples. Traffic in these unfortunates became so widespread that the Latin words for 'slave' were replaced by 'Slav', which originally denoted 'race'.

Slaves had been used by Christians under the Empire; they continued to be used on ecclesiastical estates after its fall. In 572 the Bishop of Le Mans handed over a large domain to the Abbey of St Vincent. With it went all its slaves—a married couple with a small child, four male slaves, two female and a stable boy. A similar estate was run at this time by ten slaves.

Many Christians were shocked at this traffic in human beings. In the seventh century, St Eloi, Dagobert's minister, who was very wealthy, used to buy British and Saxon slaves in batches of 50 and 100, in order to give them their freedom. Most of these were brought over by the Frisians who regularly dealt in slaves—Bede mentions a Frisian slave trader of 679 as being in London.

These unfortunates were sold privately also. In 725 we read that Ermedruda of Milan, an honourable woman, daughter of Lorenzo . . . acknowledges that she has received from Totone, most distinguished man, 12 new gold solidi as the full price for a boy of the Gallic people, named Satrelano, or by whatever other name the boy may be called. And she declared that it had come to her from her father's patrimony.

The price paid for the boy was less than that usually paid at that time for a horse. That he was regarded merely as a chattel is shown by the use of the neuter pronoun 'it' when referring to him.

The Church did not actively forbid the traffic in slaves, and in the early medieval centuries children even of Christian parents were sold. Gradually, however, this was frowned upon, and later only children of pagan parents were traded as slaves. Pope Gregory I, however, forbade the sale of Christian slaves to pagan purchasers, and King Pepin repeated his prohibition. In 845, the fate of slaves is said to have deeply moved the Fathers of the Church Council at Meaux; but their only gesture was to urge princes to stop Christian and Jewish merchants from selling them to unbelievers, since their souls might be saved if bought by Christians. Fear of the wrath of God with which delinquents were threatened would have carried far more weight then than it would today.

Commerce on a large scale took place mainly in the great international fairs of Europe. These provided centres where merchants, craftsmen and buyers could meet. The fairs of Champagne were famous from early times, but those of England, Germany and other countries became equally well known. That at St Denis, founded by Dagobert in the seventh century, grew like many others out of a religious festival. Merchants naturally gathered where there were crowds of pilgrims.

25   Scene at the fair of Lendit in Paris

The Cathedral of Notre-Dame, also in Paris, had
become—after it secured a fragment of the True Cross
in 1109—the centre of a yearly pilgrimage in June.
Soon merchants' portable booths were set up between
Montmartre and St Denis, and the fair which developed
became known as that of Lendit (from *l'endit*, an
assembly). The procession with the relic and the service
which followed, conducted by the bishop added
spiritual profit to the opportunities for worldly gain and
carnal pleasures.

Apart from these fairs, most buying and selling of
perishable goods and those for daily use took place in
weekly markets. These catered for the need of surrounding areas and were usually established by royal grants.
It was most important that prices should remain stable,
and a writer of about 900, though speaking of St
Maurillac of the fifth century, expresses contemporary
opinion when he says:

From the beginning of the episcopacy of the Blessed
Maurillac, until the end of his life, the town of

Angers—owing to his estimable qualities—enjoyed
such abundance, that the public market was never
without the produce of Ceres and Bacchus; nor did
these ever deteriorate in quality, nor increase in
price, for this would have made the poor suffer.
The sum paid for everyday produce remained
constant, so that each man had a sufficient store of
wine and wheat.

Under Otto I markets flourished in Germany in the
tenth century. The Abbey of St Vaast at Arras established one in the town and in 1036 we are given a
picture of peasants staggering into the market place
beneath loads of goods they had for sale—for no dues
were payable to the abbey on goods carried on their
owners' backs. Others, leading unshod horses, had the
satisfaction of knowing that they were saving a denier
on each animal—on shod horses two deniers were
payable. Before the stalls displaying fresh fish—
sturgeon, salmon, herring and whale meat—a pur-
veyor from a neighbouring estate might be seen, bar-
gaining for his lord; at another an overseer, buying
butcher's meat, honey, salt, oil, butter, cheese, fruit
and wine for his daughter's wedding feast; meanwhile
the girl herself, with her mother, might be haggling
over the cost of exquisitely embroidered bridal garments, or protesting shrilly when the cloth merchant,
stretching a length of famous Arras material, almost
pulled it in half in order to make it measure more. At
another stall, peasants might be inspecting knives for
pruning vines, sickles for cutting corn, or spades for
digging. Near by, a display of woad and other dyes, as
well as soles of cowhide from which shoes could be
made, would attract its own purchasers.
With the privilege of starting a market, that of
coining money was often granted. In the time of Dago-

bert, gold coins were still in circulation. But, owing to the fall in production of goods in the West, luxuries from the East had to be paid for in gold, which thus drained away into Byzantine and Moslem coffers.

It was Charlemagne who introduced the silver penny, the *denarius*, as the coin most easily negotiable for small transactions in local markets. He also introduced the system of pounds, shillings and pence with the theoretic values that $£1 = s20 = d240$ silver pennies which weighed 1 lb. Here, '$£$' is the abbreviation of '*libra*', '*s*' of '*solidus*' and '*d*' of '*denarius*'.

Although the denier of fine silver was commonly used, many people preferred to pay for purchases in kind, or partly in kind. Grasolfo, a trader, was one of these, although as a 'moneyer' he was not likely to have been short of ready cash. He had bought a piece of land in the Italian town of Lucca and in the deed of sale it is stated: 'I, the above Rodingo, son of Teodoric of blessed memory, have received as the price of that aforesaid land, which I gave you, Grasolfo, 15 gold *solidi* in cash, and 1 horse in lieu of 13 solidi, for the completion (of the purchase) of that land.'

As time went on, markets with movable stalls were replaced by ones with fixed stalls and benches, and these in turn gave way to small shops, often with vaulted store-rooms behind and living quarters above. There was a tendency for trades of one kind to be concentrated in a single area, so that, as towns and trade developed in the tenth and later centuries, there were special streets where the same kind of goods were made and sold. The Shambles was the street where butchers' shops would be found, in the Spicery spice merchants sold their wares, and in Goldsmiths' Row goldworkers plied their trade and sold their products.

But before towns and trade could develop a period of devastation began which equalled in destructive power

26 The rich merchant, Francesco Datini, and four of the poor men of
Prato
Detail from an altarpiece painted by Filippino Lippi in Prato in 1453

27   The quayside at Cologne in 1493
Woodcut from Schedel 'Weltchronik'

28   A woman at a loom
Sculpture by Pisano on the façade of the Duomo at Firenze

that of the barbarian incursions into the Roman Empire. After Charlemagne's death in 814 quarrels broke out between his successors. In addition western Christendom was attacked by enemies from outside. From the north the Vikings laid waste parts of Germany and northern France, from the east the fierce Hungarians invaded Veneto up to Padua, took Pavia, crossed the Alps into southern France, and raided Italy as far south as Otranto on her southern heel; meanwhile the Arabs, already masters of North Africa, Spain and Portugal, in 878 conquered Sicily. Even as early as the eighth century Moslems had been seizing on the trade of the Mediterranean. Their ports in Spain hummed with activity, but from Barcelona as far as Genoa and Pisa, the Frankish ports were dead and mostly deserted. Even in towns as far inland as Arles, the inhabitants had turned the Roman amphitheatre into a fortress and lived within it to be secure from Moslem raids.

But in southern Italy ports were flourishing. Amalfi, Gaeta, Salerno and Naples were by the tenth century rivalling in size and prosperity all but the larger Moslem and Byzantine cities. A contemporary writer tells us that:

> Amalfi is the most prosperous town in Lombardy, the most illustrious . . . the most affluent and opulent. Its territory borders on that of Naples. This is a fair city but less important than Amalfi. The main wealth of Naples is linen and linen cloth. I have seen pieces there the like of which I found in no other country. There is no craftsman in any other workshop in the world who is able to manufacture it.

The growing wealth of these cities, however, was not won without betrayal of their neighbours. For the sake of trade concessions, Naples and her sister cities often allied with the Moslems, even protecting and helping them to equip pirate ships preparing to raid Christian ports and merchant vessels. But, in the north, Venice was beginning to recover from the destructive effects of the Lombard conquest and the breakdown of trade-routes across the Apennines and by the sea coast. Here, as early as the ninth century, Venice had developed the system of lending out capital in order to make a profit on it. This was known at first as *commenda*, and we have the will of a wealthy Venetian, Giustiniano Partecipazio, a Doge of Venice, who refers to 'money put to work in commercial voyages'. The Doge, having chosen a merchant sailor in whose ship and leadership he had confidence, would hand to him a number of gold *solidi*. With this capital the merchant would buy slaves, wood, weapons and other goods which had been brought over the Alpine passes for sale. With these he would voyage to Constantinople, and there purchase such luxury goods as silk or purple dyes for resale at home in Venice. Here he would share the profits with Giustiniano and any other partners in the original transaction. Pisa, Genoa and other cities later adopted this form of trading.

But it was not until the eleventh and twelfth centuries that Europe was able to develop her towns and trade, during the comparative peace following the end of Viking and other raids. It was a period of extraordinary expansion and development on all fronts. Boundaries had been pushed back, new towns were established in Spain, France and Germany, new lands brought under cultivation, and more food and goods were produced; while population in-

29　Merchants bartering grain for cloth

creased. With the surplus of goods available for the first time on a substantial scale in western Europe, trade became increasingly professional. Full-time merchants and artisans operated in making and distributing goods, with markets in the Far East in view, as well as those in the Baltic and Russia.

Who were the men who took advantage of this expanding trade? In origin they were often of lowly birth. A twelfth-century romance introduces two Italian boys who from unpretentious beginnings ended as wealthy merchants with luxurious, well-staffed establishments in Ravenna and Pavia and farms in the country near by.

Sceva and Ollo were alike in age but not in character. Boys of low birth, they acquired at the same time a small capital, and in our days became first hawkers of small commodities, then by continued success, of large ones. From packmen they rose to be carriers, from that to be masters of many wagons, and always remained trusty partners.

After a time, they agreed to part, Ollo to marry a beautiful wife in Pavia, while Sceva, unmarried, settled in Ravenna. Later, Sceva visited Ollo, whom he met 'hurrying off with loaded wagons to a distant fair'. He told Sceva that he could not offer him hospitality and with scant courtesy hurried off about his business. The story has an amusing ending and shows how Ollo was punished for his lack of friendship towards his old partner.

A fact of importance is brought out in portraying Sceva and Ollo as town-dwellers. For the conduct of full-time trade it was essential that merchants should be released from feudal ties which restricted the freedom of movement and actions of those who lived on a rural domain. Many towns therefore had liberties conferred on them by a king, others by feudal princes. This led to the right of self-government—a town council of magistrates replacing traditional feudal officials as the governors of the town. In Flanders and the French royal domain during the eleventh and twelfth centuries rulers were mainly sympathetic to urban self-government. In northern Italy and north-eastern France, however, townsmen had often to struggle for their liberties, and to do so organised themselves into a 'commune'. In Laon, in 1115, a commune was formed —the king acquiescing, 'induced by a bribe from the people to confirm the same by oath'. The bishop, who had been absent in England, was filled with implacable hate against the citizens for thus freeing themselves from their feudal yoke. He persuaded the nobles to join him in offering a larger bribe to Louis VI (1108–37) than that which he had received from the townsmen. On receiving this the king agreed to annul the commune:

The compact being broken, such rage seized the citizens that all officials abandoned their duties and the stalls of the craftsmen and cobblers were closed, and nothing was exposed for sale by the innkeepers and hucksters, who expected to have nothing left when the lords began plundering. For at once the property of all was calculated by the bishops and nobles, and whatever any man had given to arrange the Commune, so much was demanded of him to procure its annulment. . . . The bishop was warned of the townspeople's fury but he took no notice.

The next day, when the bishop was engaged in business, behold there arose a disorderly noise throughout the city, men shouting, 'Commune'. . . . Then, through the middle of the chapel of the Blessed Mary . . . citizens now entered the bishop's court, with swords, battle-axes, bows and hatchets, a very great company. . . . Nobles at once rallied from all sides to the bishop. . . . Guinimon, the chatelain, an aged nobleman of handsome presence and guiltless character, armed only with shield and spear, ran into the bishop's hall and fell, struck on the back of the head by a battle-axe wielded by a certain Rainbert, his fellow-citizen. Immediately afterwards, Regnier, hurrying to enter the palace, was struck from behind with a spear and falling headlong was at once consumed by the fire of the palace from his waist downwards. . . . Next the outrageous mob, howling before the palace walls, the bishop with those who were helping him, fought them off by hurling stones and shooting arrows. For he now, as at all times, showed great spirit as a fighter. . . . But, being unable to withstand the reckless assault of the people, he put on the clothes of a servant and, flying to the vaults of the church, hid himself in a cask, shut up in which, with the head fastened on by a faithful follower, he thought himself safe. . . . But the townsmen seized a page, who refused to betray his master. Another, however, by a traitor's nod, indicated where the bishop was hidden. He was dragged from the cask by the hair and beaten. Finally, one named Bernard, lifted his battle-axe and brutally dashed out the brains of that sacred, though sinner's head.

Laon, together with Troyes, Langres and Rheims, owed much of their importance to their position as trading junctions. In these towns merchants from Italy and Provence in the south and those of Germany and from Flanders, centre of the cloth-making industry, could conveniently meet. By the twelfth century, Ypres, Ghent and Douai, with their port of Bruges, had also become great emporiums where merchants gathered to buy English wool and fine Flemish weaves. The wool of England was especially in demand on the continent and in one account we are given a glimpse of Flemish merchants crossing the Channel in company with a party of canons from Laon. Suddenly a pirate ship was sighted. The merchants, terror-struck, fell on their knees, vowing to bestow all their wealth upon Our Lady of Laon if only they were saved. Their prayer was granted but, we are told, on arrival in England, their vows forgotten, the traders travelled through England expending every penny they possessed on wool.

Many subsidiary products were needed for the manufacture of cloth, and vessels from the Mediterranean brought the prized scarlet kermes and other dye-stuffs —vermilion, lake, and brazil—from eastern lands. From northern Europe, merchants brought madder and woad to the centres of the cloth trade. But brilliant red was the most costly dye, which was why Margaret Paston, writing to her absent husband in the fifteenth century, states that she would prefer to have his presence at home 'yea, rather than a gown of scarlet'.

During the twelfth and thirteenth centuries the complicated processes of cloth-making demanded a capitalist form of organisation. Entrepreneurs like Jean Boine Broke appeared,

30   The municipal court of Paris in session

and he, in the second half of the thirteenth century, conducted a flourishing draper's business in Douai in French Flanders. We can imagine a visiting Paris merchant staying in Jean's great house which was home, office, factory and warehouse. In showing Henri his wares and establishment, Jean would begin in the sorting house. Here the humblest type of workers, wearing clogs, sorted raw wool; others washed and beat it in large tubs of water. After drying, women workers carded or combed it, according to whether the wool was long or short. It was then oiled and sent to the workers in the town or country to be spun into thread. To Henri, as he travelled about, women with distaffs, busily spinning in the fields as they minded the sheep, would be a familiar sight.

Next, the two merchants would pause to admire the skill of the warpers, arranging thread in the requisite number of strands, and cutting it to the required length; or the spoolers, winding woof-thread on to bobbins for use in the shuttle. Henri's brows would be raised as he noted that Jean had introduced a broad-loom at which two workers sat, in addition to the old-fashioned single loom for weaving narrower widths of cloth (*28*).

Fulling was done by men treading the cloth in troughs. An Arras regulation enforced that at least three men should work a single cloth since the toil was arduous, demanding 'great pain and exertion of limbs and body'. Out on the tenter ground, Jean would exchange a cheery word with 'Sarah of the Tenters'— who had worked for him for 12 years. The dripping cloths were so heavy that she had to have help in fixing them on to the hooks in the frames, so that when dry the material would be stretched to the exact size required. Near by, boys with teasels set in wooden handframes would be brushing other lengths of cloth to raise the nap, which later would be sheared by skilled workers.

The shearmen used special shears which were so highly prized by their owners that they were often bequeathed by will.

If the wool had not been dyed in the initial stages, the cloth would be taken to the dye shed and there placed in a vat containing the required shade of dye. Here, also, the workers were highly skilled as they had to know a great deal about the quality of dyestuffs, and the method of mixing colours. The cloth was pressed into the vats with special flat-ended poles, which were also used to lever the material out of the hot dye into tubs, when it was taken out to be dried once more. The final process was one of brushing with bristles set in a large square board. Then followed pressing and folding.

Jean's customers either ordered cloth to be dyed according to a special colour, or bought lengths of finished cloth from the warehouse shelves. Most of Jean's business was done through agents, some of whom were members of his own family. He was a busy man, for, in addition to his draper's business, he was immersed in the political life of Douai, and was a member of the town council no less than nine times, as well as being a leading member of his merchant guild.

Guilds were one of the most important institutions in the Middle Ages. Indeed, there were as many different sorts of guilds as there were activities. Bell-ringers and minstrels, candlemakers and grocers, road-menders and weavers—all had their guilds. They existed for charitable purposes as well as for business. When destitute or ill, a guildsman could depend on his guild for help. When he died, the guild would often pay for Masses for his soul and members were expected to attend funerals of fellow guildsmen. But guilds existed mainly to safeguard the rights of their members. They regulated prices of raw materials, and of goods for sale. They supervised work and saw to it that quality, weight and measure conformed to the necessary standard. If a member proved recalcitrant he was fined. Many guilds had their own Guild Hall where the guild officers sat to impose fines, settle quarrels or enquire about stolen goods. Later, each guild took part in the miracle plays enacted in towns on the feast days of saints. These were written round episodes in the Bible, but also contained much horseplay. In the English *Chester Deluge Play*, a great deal of rough humour is introduced when Noah's wife refuses to come into the Ark unless 'her gossips' accompany her.

> *By Christ, no! ere I see more need,*
> *Though thou stand all day and rave.*

Noah replies, no doubt to accompanying roars of laughter:

> *Lord how crabbed are women alway!*
> *They never are meek, that dare I say*
> *And that is well seen of me today*
> *In witness of you, each one.*
> *Good wife, let be all this trouble and stir*
> *That thou makest in this place here,*
> *For all men think thou art my master*
> *(And so thou art, by St John!)*

The animals all go into the ark, but Mrs Noah still stays outside drinking with her gossips:

> *Here is a bottle full of Malmsey good and strong*
> *It will rejoice both heart and tongue.*
> *Though Noah think us never so long,*
> *Here will we drink alike.*

In desperation Mrs Noah's sons hustle her into the Ark. As Noah welcomes her, she gives him a buffet on the head.

And have thou that for thy not! [Nut, head]
Aha Mary! This is hot.

In the thirteenth century, the guilds of the cloth-making industry were closing their ranks. All wage-earning artisans were excluded from membership. In Flanders and England, the 'blue-nails'—those who stained their hands with their work, weavers, fullers and dyers—were refused admission to the guild unless they ceased to work at their trade and also got rid of all necessary tools. Consequently artisans had no voice in regulating conditions, and became dependent for their livelihood and way of life on the decisions of their employers. In fact, the humbler industrial town-dwellers had little freedom. At dawn, the harsh clanging of the town bell wakened them; it rang again for their 90-minute dinner break, again for resumption of work and finally at sunset. In France, in the late four-teenth century, the king even decreed that no time should be allowed for lunch. 'If the workers wished for soup, their wives must bring it to their looms, so that work is in no wise interrupted.' Some respite was given to the workers, however, on Saturday afternoons, Sundays and Holy Days, when no work was done. Some workers in the cloth industry were employed in their own homes, and these often had employees of their own. The more skilled they were, the more independent they were likely to be, and by having their own craft guilds they were able to negotiate from strength against exploitation. But weavers and fullers remained little more than slaves, too poor even to own tools.

During the late twelfth and early thirteenth centuries Italians began to compete with the northern cloth-manufacturers in the dyeing and finishing of cloths. Florentine merchants had their shops in a street of ill-

fame called the Calima-
la. Their guild had as
its coat of arms, an eagle
clutching a corded bale
of wool in its talons. Its
merchants went to the
fairs of Champagne to
buy cloth, which they
sent by packhorse to the
Provençal ports for ship-

31   A money-changer

ment to Florence. The guilds built inns along the trade-
routes where horses were kept to maintain a swift postal
service between the fairs and the merchants' head-
quarters.

In 1350, one of these Italian merchants—Francesco
Datini—left Prato near Florence, for Avignon in
France, when only 15 years old. With an initial capital
of 150 florins he determined to make his fortune. By
1361 he was securely established in a shop in one of the
streets where the magnificent palace of Pope Clement
VI overlooked the squalid hovels of the poor. Francesco's partners were two Tuscan merchants. They sold
cuirasses, breastplates, coats of mail and other arms
imported from Milan and Como over the Alps by
packhorse. At this time soldiers of fortune, both English
and Breton, were wandering in marauding companies
through southern France after the truce of Bordeaux in
1357. In 1368, Francesco sold 64 livres' worth of arms to
Bertrand du Guesclin, commander of one of the most
famous of these companies. The previous year, Francesco had opened a shop in Barcelona, as well as
purchasing his shop in Avignon and starting a trade in
cloth, silk, spices and salt in three other shops in the
city. Not content with this, he set up as a money-
changer, dealing also in works of art, jewellery and
silver goods. His main shop in Avignon held a dazzling

display of armour, silver belts, tooled leather goods, saddles and mule harness from Cordova, linen from Genoa, scarlet silks from Lucca, silk curtains, white, blue and woollen cloth from Florence.

Fine, painted dowry-chests were also in demand. An order for one of these states that:

> it must be of medium size . . . for a lady, painted on a vermilion or azure ground, according to what you can find. Let them be handsome and showy, of good workmanship, and made of light, dry wood . . . the finer and better they are, the better I can sell them.

That the slave trade was still thriving in the four-teenth century is clear from Francesco's letter to his foster-mother about his proposed visit to Prato:

> Place not garlic before me, or leeks or roots. Make home a Paradise to me, I refuse to be still treated as a boy. . . . Tell me if you need a slave or other wench. . . . If you would have a slave, I will send one young and fair, skilled in every matter, who will not bring shame upon the house.

During the thirteenth century the slave trade had declined, but labour shortages following the Black Death revived a demand for them. They came from Spain, Africa, Constantinople, Cyprus, Crete and the shores of the Black Sea. By the end of the fourteenth century most wealthy households in Italy had at least one slave.

We hear many tales of them escaping during voyages, but of 12 Moorish captives who made the attempt only two were successful: 'One named Dmitri, a big hand-some fellow with a rosy complexion, the other sallow, lacking a front tooth.' Their owner wrote that they were roaming about in Provence and begged that a look-out should be kept for them. If caught, he directed, they should be returned to him by boat, 'strongly fettered'.

Like other wealthy merchants of this period, Francesco built himself a grand house, with vaulted chambers, fine fireplaces, large bedrooms, but no latrines or bathrooms, though in the chief guest-rooms and hall there were commodes, and also basins for washing the feet, with one barber's basin in the kitchen. Not many could afford stone houses, however. The poor lived in mud hovels and better dwellings were of wood, thatched and highly inflammable. By this later period tiles were being used and some glazed windows. Italian nobles had fortified towers within the towns which, throughout western Europe, were guarded by walls with strong gateways.

Life within a medieval town had many disadvantages. Streets were narrow and airless, since the projecting storeys of opposite buildings almost met overhead. Fires were constantly breaking out. The stench from open gutters, innumerable dung-heaps and refuse flung into the roadway was overpowering. Pigs were left to roam the streets and noise was as great a nuisance as in ancient or modern towns. We read of a student in Germany who was permitted to remove from his house a smith whose incessant hammering disturbed his studies; of another, who 'compelled a certain weaver who filled the neighbourhood with songs and shouting, almost without cessation, to change his lodging. Nevertheless the fellow continued to make a terrible noise.' At Jena, also, 'a certain cooper used to get up at midnight and made so much din putting hoops on his casks' that the health of his neighbours was imperilled through constant loss of sleep. Small wonder then that Francesco Datini, like other wealthy merchants, put money into farms and land so that they could escape at times from the feuds, noise and stench of the towns.

But Francesco, although wealthy, was not one of the

32   Masons at work

circle of the great international trading companies whose ancestors had, in 1293, seized from the landed nobles control of the state. Soon the new commercial magnates had adopted the social outlook of the feudal lords they had ousted, and formed a new aristocracy. By 1300 the great office-holders in Venice were already patrician in character. Their old, blind and wily Doge, Enrico Dandolo had, by imposing his own terms on the leaders of the Fourth Crusade, secured for Venice the domination of the Four Seas—the Adriatic, the Aegean, the Sea of Marmora and the Black Sea. For the same Crusaders in 1204 captured Constantinople and, by the terms of their treaty with Venice, had to hand over rich ports and islands which established the commercial supremacy of the Italian city over her former rival.

The ceremonial that surrounded the appointment of a Doge—the supreme ruler of Venice—even in 1268 was designed to impress all who beheld it with the splendour and wealth of the city. Through the eyes of Martin da Canal, who was present, we can watch the celebrations, see the Grand Canal sparkling in the sunshine and on its waters 50 galleys, sails billowing in the wind. On their decks crews cheered and shouted themselves hoarse. Meanwhile the guilds advanced across the Piazza of St Mark—the master-smiths garlanded, with banners flying, heralded by trumpets; then the furriers splendid in samite and scarlet silk; weavers, richly decked, with ten master tailors in white, decorated with crimson stars. Next came the master-clothmakers, the fustian- and quilt-makers, led by children singing *chansonettes*. Resplendent in cloth of gold, . the clothmakers marched

33 A harpist and lutenist

attended by servants in gold and purple. Many other guilds followed, all gorgeously arrayed, each with its own band. On reaching the Doge and Dodaressa, they shouted, 'Long live our lord, the noble Doge Lorenzo Tiepolo'.

For a week rejoicings continued—different bodies and guilds paying their tribute to the Doge, but to Venice also, for were not its palaces and churches, its ceremonies, its bejewelled citizens, its wealth and splendour, all reflections of the pride and power of the greatest trading city in the world?

But with the fourteenth century Europe entered a period of crisis and decline. In France, the Hundred Years War had ruined her prosperity. At its end, however, Charles VII, aided by a commercial genius— Jacques Coeur, the son of a tanner of Bourges—set about rebuilding French commerce. Not only did Jacques organise a fleet to bring luxury goods from the East, but he established a silk manufactory in Florence, dyeworks and papermills in France, and, by restarting the French mines at a period when metal was being

widely used, even for household utensils, he revived the
trade of France.

This splendour of ceremonial in Venice, and the
revival of trade in France, which brought shiploads of
luxury goods from the East, were but single facets of
the growing richness and extravagance of everyday
life. The owners of elegant stone-built houses, like those
of Datini and Jacques Coeur, showed an equal ostenta-
tion in the magnificence of their dress, all reflections of
the increasing wealth and licence of the times. Men, as
well as women, adopted extreme fashions. Women's
head-dresses became absurdly high and pointed. Made
of gold and silver tissue they were much bejewelled.
Their long, fur-trimmed velvet and brocade gowns,
heavy and cumbersome, might seem to point to a lack
of activity on the part of wealthy ladies. Yet a detailed
examination of the lives of women and wives of every
class, prove that in the majority of cases this conclusion
is wrong. Most of them, in fact, played no small or easy
part in promoting the wealth and prosperity, the
culture and learning of western Europe, throughout the
Middle Ages.

4

WOMEN AND WIVES

'WOMEN in the Middle Ages found themselves per-
petually oscillating between a pit and pedestal.' The
Church's view, when broadcast by monks, clergy and
friars preaching the ascetic ideal, was that woman was an
instrument of the Devil, the supreme temptress, and as
such must necessarily be both evil and inferior to
man. How then did this teaching react in the sphere of
everyday life? Here, from necessity, women's actual
condition varied not only from century to century but,
much more, from class to class. The well-born woman's
lot differed from that of the rich merchant's wife, and
both even more from the position of villeins and serfs.
Yet most men—theoretically at least—agreed that
women were inferior beings. This gave them the right
to inflict corporal punishment upon them.

There is ample proof of this attitude. A Dominican,
Nicolas Byard, declared in the thirteenth century: 'A
man may chastise his wife and beat her for correction,
for she is of his household, therefore the lord may chastise
his own.' Canon Law also stated: 'It is plain that wives
should be subject to their husbands and should almost
be servants.' Even the kindly and affectionate Goodman
of Paris told his wife in the fourteenth century to

copy the behaviour of a dog who always has his
heart and his eye upon his master; even if his master
whip him and throw stones at him, the dog follows,

wagging his tail. . . . Wherefore for a better and
stronger reason, women ought to have a perfect and
solemn love for their husbands.

In Customary Law and Practice in the thirteenth
century one clause of the statutes of a new town in
Gascony asserted: 'All inhabitants of Villefranche have
the right to beat their wives, provided they do not kill
them thereby.' The Knight of La Tour-Landry, in his
famous book written to give advice to his daughters,
tells them of an aristocratic wife who, by scolding her
husband in public, so incensed him that he 'smote her
with his fist down to the earth, then with his foot he
kicked her face and broke her nose . . . so that ever after
she was shamed to show her visage, it was so foul
blemished.'

At the opposite end of the social scale, village women
who dared to rail against their husbands were doused
in the ducking stool in the village pond. Court rolls
show that villages were repeatedly threatened or fined
for failing to provide these punitive instruments. But in
justice it should be remembered that spouse-beating
was not entirely the privilege of the male sex. Chaucer's
Wife of Bath, a brilliant portrayal of a woman of that
particular type and class, in recalling the suffering she
had inflicted on three of her previous husbands, cried
joyfully, 'O Lord! the pain I did them and the wo'.
Misericords and manuscript illuminations tell the same
story.

Womankind was also regarded with gratitude and
pity in, at least some, male quarters. A French poem
declares:

> *Much ought woman to be held dear.*
> *By her is everybody clothed.*
> *Woman spins and makes our garments*
> *Of cloth of gold and cloth of silk.*

> *To all who read this story I say,*
> *Speak no ill of womankind.*

A fifteenth-century writer sets out to champion the working woman:

> *A woman is a worthy thing,*
> *They do the wash and do the wring.*
> *'Lullay, lullay', she doth sing,*
> *And yet she hath but care and woe.*
>
> *A woman is a worthy wight,*
> *She serveth man both day and night,*
> *Thereto she putteth all her might,*
> *And yet she hath but care and woe.*

Perhaps it was in the sphere of marriage that women's lot was the hardest, bearing on them more severely the lower their position in the social scale. Marriages were seldom a matter of choice but of arrangement by parents, guardians and overlords. The over-riding consideration was financial gain or territorial aggrandisement. In the case of villeins their owners arranged for their early marriage since their offspring belonged to their overlord and their increase brought more workers for his estates.

The great lady, however, had not necessarily any better chance of a happy marriage than the bondwoman at her gates. Johann Busch, the fifteenth-century Saxon reformer, has drawn a pathetic picture of the Duchess of Brunswick on her death-bed:

When her confession with absolution and penance was ended, I said to her, 'Think you lady, that you will pass to the kingdom of heaven when you die?' She replied, 'This believe I firmly.' Said I, 'That would be a marvel. You were bred in castles and for many years have lived with your husband the Lord

Duke amid innumerable delights, with wine and ale, meat and venison, both roast and boiled; and yet you expect to fly away to heaven directly you die.'

She answered, 'Beloved father, why should I not now go to heaven? I have lived in this castle like an anchoress in a cell. What delights or pleasures have I had here, save that I have endeavoured to show a happy face to my servants and maidens? I have a hard husband, as you know, who has hardly any care or inclination towards women. Have I not been in this castle as it were in a cell?'

I said to her, 'You think then that God will send his angels when you die, to bear your soul to Paradise?'

'This believe I firmly', she replied. Then said I, 'May God give you what you believe.'

The woman serf, however, fared worse, being regarded as little more than a beast. In 1411, on the manor of Liestal near Basle, it was prescribed that 'every year before Shrove Tuesday, when folk are accustomed to think of holy matrimony, the bailiff shall consider what boys and girls are of such an age that they may take wife or husband, so that he may allot to each his mate'.

Queen Blanche, mother of St Louis, pitied the serfs so much that she ordained that in many places they should be freed and pay some other due. She had most compassion for the young girls in serfdom, for men would not take them in marriage, and many of them were deflowered. This reluctance to marry serfs caused not only hardship but tragedy in the case of a poor servant girl of Champagne. In 1472 she was convicted of child murder but pleaded that she had been prevented by her father from marrying 'the man she would gladly have taken', because he was a serf. On the other

34 Christine de Pisan presents a book of her poems to Isabel of
Bavaria, Queen of France
Miniature from an early fifteenth-century French manuscript

35   A game of chess
Ivory carving on the back of a mirror

36   A country dance
Miniature from an English manuscript

hand, on some estates a more humane attitude was taken towards bondwomen especially during their confinements, when they were sometimes excused the annual tribute of the Shrovetide hen, or received the gift of a load of firewood or fish from the lord's pond.

At Denchendorff in Germany each female serf received two measures of wine and eight white loaves at the christening of each of her children. As Christine de Pisan, a medieval woman writer, states, 'They received bread, milk, lard and potage, also some fish, and their life was often more secure and even more satisfying than that of better born women.'

The Church's attitude towards divorce did not make woman's lot more enviable. According to Canon Law a marriage, once made, was unbreakable. The furthest the Church would go was to make a marriage 'null and void', to say that a true marriage had never taken place. Relationship within the fourth degree made a marriage spiritually unlawful. So that by fabricating a false ancestry, a man, if tired of his wife, or for any other reason, could get rid of her, provided he could afford the expense of the necessary proceedings.

A satirical poem of the time of Edward II tells us:

> *If a man have a wife,*
> *And he love her not,*
> *Bring her to the consistory court.*
> *There truth should be wrought.*
> *Bring two false witnesses with him,*
> *And himself the third,*
> *And he shall be separated*
> *As far as he would bide from his wife;*
> *He shall be backed up full well*
> *To lead a disreputable life.*

The discovery of servile ancestry in a wife was also a sufficient cause to annul a marriage; while some, having spent their wife's fortune, 'shamelessly deserted her, delighting in a prudent, handsomer and wealthier mate'.

Yet there is abundant evidence of happy marriages. The Goodman of Paris—an elderly French official of wealth and position—wrote a book of instructions for his child-wife, an orphan. Throughout the many pages, his sympathy and loving understanding for her keeps breaking through. He tells her that he writes the book

> for your honour and love and not for my service, since I had pity and loving compassion on you, who for long have had neither father nor mother to whom you might turn for counsel in your need, save me alone. . . . And know that I am pleased that you tend rose-trees and care for violets, and make chaplets and dance and sing. . . . As for the greater service you say you would willingly do me, if you were able and I taught it you, know, dear sister, that I am well content that you should do me such service as your good neighbours of like estate do for their husbands. . . . For I am not so overweening in my attitude to you that I am not satisfied with what you do for me. Provided there be no scorn or disdain. For although I know well you are of gentler birth than I, . . . yet in you I have no fear, I have confidence in your good intent.

Throughout his book the Goodman adopts this almost humble tone—'for to me belongeth none save the common service, or less'.

Thomas Betson, a 40-year-old English merchant who traded in Calais, was deeply in love with his fiancée of 15, Katherine Riche, as we can plainly see from his letter to her in 1476:

> My own heartily beloved Cousin Katherine, I recommend me to you with all my heart. The token

you sent is most welcome to me. Also a letter from your gentle squire telling me you are in good health and merry at heart. . . . If you would be a good eater of your meat alway, that you might grow fast to be a woman, you should make me the gladdest man of the world. . . .

I pray you greet well my horse and beg him to give you four of his years to help you. And at my coming I will give him four of my years and four horse loaves. Tell him that I prayed him so. . . . And Almighty Jesu make you a good woman. . . . At great Calais, the first day of June, when every man was gone to his dinner, and the clock smote nine, and all your household cried after me and bade me 'Come down to dinner at once!' and what answer I gave them, you know of old.

By your faithful lover and Cousin, Thomas Betson. I send you this ring for a token.

Thomas Betson continued to wish that his Katherine would make haste and grow to marriageable age, for two years later he wrote to her mother: 'I remember Katherine full oft, God knows. I dreamed once she was thirty winters of age, and when I woke I wished she had been but twenty, and so by likelihood I am sooner like to have my wish than my dream.' Soon after, Thomas married his Katherine and we know she proved a loving and helpful wife. For when, a year later,

37   An espousal

Thomas fell dangerously ill, Katherine, though but 16
and expecting the birth of her eldest son, not only
nursed him faithfully, but looked after his business with
all the competence to which the medieval women and
the upper classes were trained from early childhood.

The Knight of La Tour-Landry, in spite of his
horrifying account of the harsh treatment accorded to a
managing wife, of which he obviously approved, had
clearly himself been most happily married. At the
beginning of his book he writes that he had had

> a wife that was both fair and good . . . and loved
> songs, ballads and rondels and diverse new things.
> But death, that on all makes war, took her from me,
> which has made me have many a sorrowful thought
> and great heaviness. And so it is more than xx year
> that I have been for her full of great sorrow. For a
> true lover's heart never forgets the woman that once
> he hath truly loved.

This more idealistic view of women was strengthened
by the growth during the twelfth century of the cult of
the Virgin. Together with the adoration given to the
Mother of Our Lord there developed the idea of the
superiority of womanhood. One medieval writer
explicitly states:

> Woman is to be preferred to man, to wit: in material,
> because Adam was made from clay, and Eve from
> Adam's side; in place, because Adam was made
> outside Paradise and Eve within; in conception
> because a woman conceived God, which man could
> not do; in apparition, because Christ appeared to a
> woman after the resurrection; in exaltation, because
> a woman is exalted above the choirs of angels, to wit,
> the Blessed Mary.

On the mundane side, the cult of the Virgin was balanced by the cult of the lady, as followed by the knights of medieval chivalry. This was a secular, not an ecclesiastical, invention. But the two cults grew together, each helping to counteract the ascetic view of woman which detracted from her worth and actually defamed her. The

38   Painting a statuette of the Virgin

lyrical poetry of the troubadours and minnesingers of France and Germany who, using love and worship of the lady as their central themes, also aimed at elevating both emotions to the high position they held in the orders of chivalry:

When the days lengthen in the month of May
Well pleased am I to hear the birds
Sing far away.

And when from that place I am gone,
I hang my head to make dull moan,
Since she my heart is set upon
Is far away.

Yet shall I know no other love but hers,
And if not hers, no other love at all
She hath surpassed all.
So fair she is, so noble—I would be
A captive in the hosts of paynimrie
In a far land, if so be upon me,
Her eyes might fall.

It will not be, for at my birth they said,
That one had set this doom upon my head,
—God curse him among men—
That I should love, and not till I be dead,
Be loved again.

The whole business of courtly love was organised as strictly as feudalism itself. A formal ceremony took place when a lover was accepted, following the lines of the payment of homage by a vassal to his lord. The lover knelt, his two hands joined between his lady's hands, then, before witnesses, he swore to serve her faithfully till death, and to defend her against all assailants. Accepting his services, the lady promised him her tenderest affection, put a ring on his finger, kissed him, then raised him to his feet.

Courts of love were also established in which romantic matters were tried. The judges were ladies. Even scholars in the universities prided themselves on their knowledge of the subtleties of love, and praised their chosen ladies in rhymes and verses.

39   A lover's homage

Take thou this rose, O rose,
Since love's own flower it is,
And by that rose
Thy lover captive is.

may well have been a fragment from Abelard's pen,
expressing the 'shattering ecstasy' of his love for
Héloïse.

Less realistic was a certain mock church council held
in the mid-twelfth century. Modelled on the lay Courts
of Love it was posed the problem of deciding whether it
is better to be loved by a clerk than a cavalier. Two
ladies, Elizabeth de Fauçon and Elizabeth de Granges,
upheld the courtly and honourable loves of clerks. The
ladies were garlanded with the blossoms of May—
gillyflowers, lilies, roses and violets—and sang love-
songs to open the session. It was finally decided that
clerks—discreet and courtly—were preferable as lovers
to the swash-buckling knight, who tended boastfully
to blazon his love abroad.

The most famous poem about romantic love was the
Romance of the Rose which was widely read throughout
Europe from the thirteenth to the fifteenth centuries.
In the form of an allegory, it was written by a poet of the
Loire valley—Guillaume de Lorris—who died before
he could complete the work. Forty years later another
writer of different calibre, Jean de Meun, undertook
the task. Jean's section contains bitter attacks on love
and women, two of his couplets being well-known:

Of honest women, by St Denis
There are fewer than of phoenixes

and

You are, will be or have been
Unchaste in fact or will.

They form part of a violent satire on marriage and probably reflect the attitude, not only of de Meun himself, but of many men of the fourteenth and fifteenth centuries.

At the end of the fourteenth century, however, Christine de Pisan took up the championship of her sex in her *Epistle to the God of Love* which defended women against the aspersions of the *Romance of the Rose*. Christine was one of the few women writers of the Middle Ages whose work brought them lasting fame. She was the daughter of an Italian—Thomas de Pisan—who was invited by Charles V of France to go to Paris in 1368 as court astrologer. Christine was well educated, then at 15 married a Frenchman, who, dying in the terrible plague of 1402, left her with three young children and other relatives to support. Christine, who had already composed many poems and major works, decided to become a professional writer.

40   Spinning, carding and weaving wool

An illustration in a manuscript of one of her books portrays Christine presenting her work to Isabelle of Bavaria, queen of Charles VI. The young writer and the staid queen are so realistically painted that they must almost certainly be authentic portraits. The scene is Isabelle's bedroom, with its blue *fleur-de-lys* hangings, rich carpets and two beds with sumptuous silken red covers. The queen's lapdog reclines on the bed behind her while a larger hound keeps guard near the door. Christine kneels to present her huge volume bound in scarlet leather, while the six seated ladies in waiting, with their horned head-dresses, stare curiously or impassively on. We have here, most probably, the first portrait of a professional woman writer of western Europe (*34*).

There were many aristocratic poetesses among the twelfth-century troubadours of southern France. The Countess of Provence, the Countess of Die, Clair d'Anduze, Adelaide de Porcairgues and the Dame Capelloza, all wrote in praise of their lovers.

During the following century in the north of France, poems ascribed to the Duchess of Lorraine and the Dame de la Fayel are still extant. But in the thirteenth century Marie de France, who seems to have settled in England, won more durable fame than any of these by writing *lais*. These were romantic poems based on ancient romances similar to those about Arthur and Charlemagne. Marie claimed that the first of her *lais* was based on Breton legends. Her most popular book was a translation of English fables into French. This she undertook, she tells us, for love of William Longespée, Earl of Salisbury, the son of the English Henry II by Fair Rosamunde.

But most women, even of the aristocratic class, had to occupy themselves with more practical affairs. An outstanding characteristic of medieval wives was their capacity to deal not only with the management of their households—a complicated enough matter in itself— but also to undertake the running of their husbands' estates during their absence on crusade, at the wars, or in the courts, dealing with legal disputes that arose so often in medieval times.

They also acted as hostess in the lord's absence,

meeting guests as they emerged through the outer
gateway into the castle courtyard. One romance tells
us of the Count d'Artois' visit to the Countess of
Boulogne, who with her fair daughter meets him and
his squire in the outer court and conducts him to the hall
where dancing and singing are provided for his
entertainment. It was equally necessary to conduct the
parting guest to the gate. In the *Romance of the Violet*,
Gerard of Nevers, the hero who has delivered his
host and family from the persecutions of a giant, is
taking a sudden leave. The daugher of the castle, who
loves Gerard, hearing of his departure, jumps from bed
and

> runs to him, in her mere *bliault* [a sort of dressing
> gown], without wimple, or chaplet of gold on her
> head, which nevertheless shines fairer than gold. The
> fresh colours of her face are lovely as a rose on a May
> morning, her body is well made and graceful. With
> her slender hands she lifted her robe revealing a foot,
> white and small, delicate and clean.

It also devolved upon the lady of the castle to train
not only her own young children but also older girls
sent for that purpose from neighbouring castles and
great houses. They were expected to behave demurely,
not to talk too much, to be courteous and modest
before gentlemen, when walking not to trot or run. As
one code of instruction has it, 'Running and trotting,
your own heart will tell you, are not becoming in a
lady.' The Knight of La Tour-Landry and the Goodman of Paris both stress the necessity of correct deport-
ment. When sitting, the hands must be folded on the lap
or breast, the eyes modestly turned down.

Spinning, weaving and the making of clothes, were
skills possessed by practically all women in the Middle
Ages. The art of *orfrois*, embroidering in gold and silver,

was not so common.
From one *fabliau* we
learn of the daughter
of a knight, 'noble and
courteous, who placed
his daughter with a bur-
gher, who taught her to
work *orfrois* along with
his own daughter'. Por-
traits of friends and
lovers were sometimes
stitched on to rich silk,
and, as a mark of
special attachment, a

41 Home dressmaking

damsel would weave strands of her own hair into the
design.

Women were also taught the use of medicinal herbs
and became skilled in massage and simple first aid.
They were not allowed to practise outside the home as
doctors or surgeons. The medieval illustration of Tobit,
lying blind and ill on his settle while his wife Anna
prepares medicine for him, mirrors many contemporary
scenes (*85*). Anna has a book, no doubt of medical
'receipts' on her knee, so she could obviously read. The
numerous copies of such medical books that still
remain testify to their frequent use in the Middle Ages.

In the matter of household management, *bourgeois*
and upper-class women excelled. As cooks, they were
experts, and even though servants were numerous, they
were expected to supervise them and had therefore to
have a thorough knowledge of every household task
themselves. Medieval dishes were strongly seasoned so
that pepper, cloves, garlic, cinnamon and vinegar,
verjuice and wine are found in many of the recipes. Ale
was frequently used, especially for cooking fish.
Almonds were cooked with meat, as well as in sweets,

42   Dining in state with musicians, cup-bearers and a carver

and saffron was useful for colouring especially if, 'the eggs used do not make the mixture yellow enough'. The Goodman of Paris gave his wife detailed directions on the ordering of dinners and suppers which included warnings against burning the potage: 'Item, before your potage burns, stir it often at the bottom of the pot. And *note*, as soon as you perceive the potage burning, straightway take it off the fire and put in another pot.'

The amount of materials used in making medieval dishes would astound the modern housewife. For frumenty, the Goodman directed that 100 eggs should be beaten into each eight pints of milk; for one egg dish with herbs, 16 eggs were to be beaten, to which were added chopped dittany, rue, tansy, mint, sage, marjoram, fennel, parsley, beets, violet leaves, spinach, lettuce and pounded ginger. Such a mixture of strong flavours must have been overpowering!

Many birds that are not usually eaten today were served up at banquets—swans, cranes, herons, peacocks and even gulls were included in the menu.

In addition to the actual preparation of food, the housewife had to buy large supplies in advance. Much of the food had to be preserved in autumn, as many cattle were killed off before the winter and the meat salted down for later use. Fish for salting had also to be bought at the appropriate time. Richard Calle, the bailiff of the English Paston family, wrote to Margaret Paston:

> Mistress, it were good to remember your stuff of herring now this fishing time. I have got me a friend in Lowestoft to help buy me seven or eight barrel and they shall not cost more than 6s. 8d. a barrel. You shall do more now (autumn) with 40s. than you shall do at Christmas with 5 marks (66s. 8d.).

Dried cod was also bought in quantity and salted down.

Foreign goods had to be bought from the nearest large town. Margaret Paston, writing to her son in London, asks him to find out the cost of pepper, cloves, mace, ginger, cinnamon, almonds, rice and saffron, also of raisins and 'galingal'. Galingal was an aromatic root from the East Indies which the Good-man of Paris told his wife should have a reddish-violet hue when cut, 'that which is heavy and firm to the knife, like a nut, is good'. This root was also used as a medicine. We can see the young Parisienne, after poring over her husband's directions on how to buy food for dinners, setting out with Agnes, the housekeeper, on a shopping expedition, with servants behind to carry the goods.

In the nearest market they would buy Corbeil bread, also trencher bread, half-a-foot wide and four inches high, baked four days before. 'And let it be brown', the

young wife would say, remembering the Goodman's
injunctions.

Then to the butcher's for half a mutton to make soup,
with a quarter of bacon to enrich it, some veal and
venison. From the poulterer 10 capons and 10 ducklings
and 10 rabbits to roast, with a lean pig to make jelly
for them. From the spicer, pounds of different spices.
Then again, the wife whispers, 'And 2 lb. of large and
small candles.' The spicer smiles and adds 6*s*. 8*d*. to the
bill.

From the milk market 'a sester of good milk, neither
curdled nor watered to make frumenty'; in the Place de
Greve Agnes orders a hundred Burgundy faggots to be
sent to the house and two sacks of coal at 10*s*. At the
Porte de Paris they come on a flower stall and buy
greenery, violets and gillyflowers. So they go on, until,
tired and hungry, they return home, the young wife a
shade more sophisticated than she had been, having
put into practice some of her husband's precepts.

It is seldom that we can meet medieval servants face
to face but we do so for a brief moment as we step inside
a Franco-Flemish *bourgeois* house of the fourteenth
century. Here the mistress is about to instruct Janet,
her servant.

'Janet, listen to me.' 'What am I to listen to . . . I am
busy.' 'And what are you doing?' 'I am making the
beds, setting straight the cushions on forms, benches,
tuffets and stools, and I am cleaning the solar
[parlour], the chamber, the house and kitchen.'
'You're a good girl and I praise you, but tell Jehan
he is slow.' 'Where is he ma'am?' 'How do I know? I
expect by your side. He seems ready enough to
follow you round about the beds when you are
alone.' 'Saint Mary, ma'am, what are you talking
about? Upon my oath, he hates nothing so much as

me.' Then Janet tells a story about Jehan which
shows his intentions are anything but honourable.
'Oh Dieu!' the mistress exclaims, 'Janet, are you as
innocent as you make out? Come down. Bring towels,
linen and coal. Blow up the fire. Take the tongs and
mend it so that it burns. Boil the pots, fry some fat,
lay the table and bring the long cloth, put water in
the hand basin.' 'Madam, where are the copper, the
cauldron and our pans?' 'Are you blind? They are
beside the cupboard.'

In the same way we are shown first-hand pictures of ·
fourteenth-century women of the gentry class, through
various contemporary accounts. A knowledge of law
was as important to a wife in those litigious days as to
her husband. In 1465, Margaret Paston was called upon
to defend her husband's interests during his absence
against so important an adversary as the Duke of
Suffolk. The Paston manor of Drayton had been un-
lawfully claimed by the Duke. Margaret fought him
through the local courts and wrote to John Paston:

> Right worshipful husband, it were well done that you
> should speak with the Justices ere they come here.
> If you will that I complain to them, if God fortune
> me, I will do as you advise, for in good faith . . . what
> with sickness and trouble that I have had, I am
> brought right low and weak, but to my power I will
> do as I can or may in your matters.

Soon after this, her husband was flung into the Fleet
Prison. Yet Margaret, still full of spirit, in spite of
bodily weakness, rose early one morning and sought an
interview with the judges before they left for the Shire
House. The Duke's officers had arrested one of her
men. Margaret told them all the circumstances. The
judges at once gave the Duke's bailiff 'a passing great

rebuke'. Later the imprisoned servant was set free, the Duke's officers were still further censured, and all demands against the Pastons overridden. Margaret, overjoyed, wrote at once to her husband so excited that she tells part of her story twice over!

On an earlier occasion Margaret was besieged in another manor she was defending against the Lord Moleyns, when

> the said Lord sent to the mansion a riotous people, to the number of a thousand persons . . . arrayed in manner of war with cuirasses, coats of mail, steel helmets, bows and arrows, large shields, guns, pans with fire, long cromes to draw down houses, ladders and picks with which they mined down the walls, and long trees, with which they broke up gates and doors.

All this time, Margaret was in the house with only 12 other persons. The attackers drove out her companions, but Margaret, knowing that 'possession was nine points of the law', shut herself into a small inner chamber. She refused to leave and had finally to be borne out at the gates, when the 'riotous people' proceeded to wreck and rifle the mansion 'bearing away stuff, array and money to the value of £200' (about £16,000 of present-day money).

Even under peaceful conditions the life of the landed proprietor's wife was busy enough, for the great lady was expected to have a watchful eye upon the manorial workers:

> Let her go often into the fields to see how they are working . . . and let her make them get up in the morning. If she be a good housewife, let her rise herself, throw on a *houppelande* [a fourteenth-century outer garment] and go to the window and shout until

she see them come running out, for they are given to laziness.

After breaking her fast we see her again striding in country clothes through the coppices, the cornfields and pastures, casting an observant eye on horses and cattle, for even the young wife of the Goodman, living in Paris, was supposed to know everything about the management of her husband's farm. He tells her:

When you are in the country I bid Agnes the Béguine [the house-keeper] order those whose business it is to take thought for the beasts. Thus Robin the shepherd should look to his sheep, Josson the oxherd to his oxen and bulls, Arnold the cowherd and Jehanneton the dairymaid take thought for the kine, the heifers and calves, the sows, pigs and piglings, Eudeline the farmer's wife look to the geese, goslings, cocks, hens, chickens, doves and pigeons and the carter or the farmer care for the horses and mares. For the said Béguine and you likewise ought to show your folk that you know about it all and care about it, for so they will be the more diligent.

We are relieved at last to find the Goodman writing, 'Now I am in mind to let you rest or disport you' and to follow the child wife as she walks sedately, her hands crossed, out into the garden. For this was one of the favourite retreats of medieval women. The Goodman had also assured her that it pleased him that she should dance and sing. Indeed all medieval women delighted in these pleasures, peasants and great ladies alike. Village dancing, undoubtedly pagan in origin, often led to excesses and was frowned upon by the Church. Usually the same woman in each village was the leader of the dance and marked the time by ringing a small bell. The singing of ballads in castle-hall, local alehouse or market square was a popular pastime. One strange legend about dancing was first recorded as a ballad in a German chronicle of 1013. It concerns a priest and his family and tells how 'Upon a Christmas night, Twelve fools a carol dight'. A carol was the name then given to a dance accompanied by a song. It must be remembered that at this period, and indeed for long after, the canon law forbidding priests to marry was not always strictly observed.

These 'fools' tempted the priest's daughter to join them in dancing round the church just as her father was about to perform the Mass. The priest forbade the dance and begged the merry-makers to come in to the service. They refused, and one cried, 'Why standë we, why go we not?' and the mad dance began again. Angered now, the priest prayed 'to God, that he on believed' that they should dance without ceasing until twelve months were past. As the dancers rushed by, the priest's son seized his sister's arm. To his horror it broke off like a dead branch, but all danced on.

> *All that yearë, hand in hand,*
> *Night nor day they wist of none,*
> *When it was come, when it was gone . . .*
> *But ever sang they the song they wrought,*
> *'Why standë we, why go we not?'*

At last the period of the curse was ended:

> *In the twinkling of an eye,*
> *Into the church gan they to fly,*
> *And on the pavement fell they down,*
> *As they were dead or fall'n in swoon.*

Other less tragic dances took place in the country; on festivals such as May Day and Midsummer Day, at sheep-shearings and harvest homes. Then the tunes would be played by a man performing on an instrument like bagpipes (*36*).

Working women and burghers' wives loved also to resort to the alehouse, often kept by a woman who brewed the ale. Here they exchanged gossip and stories. Farces, which were written to enliven the 'mystery' or religious plays, show us many vignettes of alehouse scenes. One portrays the meeting of a yeoman's and a sergeant's wife. The former announces that the sergeant's arm has just been broken in a scuffle. 'Oh!' cried the injured man's wife. 'He beat me sorely last night. I am glad he is hurt.'

They go to an inn to celebrate the good news. 'You shall drink first, gossip,' says the sergeant's wife. 'You brought the news of my husband's evil plight. Would that his head were broken entire, then he could beat me no more.'

Another popular place was the public bath. By the first half of the thirteenth century these had been reintroduced to the main cities of Europe through the influence of returned Crusaders. Built on the Moslem pattern, these included hot steam baths; they were also patronised by both men and women as social clubs. These finally became so disreputable that, by 1546, they were suppressed in England, though they continued in France and other countries until a later period.

Upper-class women spent a good deal of time playing chess (*35*) and other board games. Draughts or 'dames' was popular, though not as exciting as 'tables' which was played with dice. The Goodman describes town ladies engaged in indoor games like blind man's buff. Ball games were indulged in out-of-doors and picnics in summer were organised when flowers were gathered and chaplets and garlands woven from them. May Day was an occasion for expeditions to the country by boat, on horseback, on foot, by horse litter and

43   Women stag hunting

perhaps even by 'char'. This was such a cumbersome vehicle, however, being drawn by a long team of horses, that it was mainly reserved for longer journeys. It was luxuriously fitted with cushions and awnings, and was large enough to transport a queen or great lady with all her chief attendants.

Medieval women were almost as much addicted to outdoor sports as men. John of Salisbury condemns the practice of hunting and reproves the eagerness with which women also joined in the chase. The hare, the hart, the wolf and the boar, as well as the buck, doe, fox, martin and roe, were all hunted. Several sorts of hounds were used, among them the rache, or scenting hound, and the greyhound. An early poem tells us of a lady setting out for the chase:

> She was as fair and as good,
> And as rich on her palfrey;
> Her greyhounds filled with the deer's blood,
> Her raches coupled, by my faith.

In the illustration, the lady riding astride is blowing her horn, her attendant shooting at a stag which the hound is attacking. It required considerable skill to blow a horn. It was used to convey orders to the hounds, rather in the way a modern sheepdog manoeuvres in response to his owner's whistles. Certain notes also conveyed that the hart had been sighted and carried orders to the huntsmen in the chase. Ladies hunted the hare with bow and arrow and the rabbit with ferrets; they also loved hawking and fishing.

Dress, as in all ages, formed one of the chief interests of medieval women, especially those of the upper classes. Sumptuary laws forbade the middle and lower classes to indulge in any richness of dress, even had they been able always to afford it. In the *Romance of the Rose* the dress of the Lady Riches is described:

> *Riches had a robe of purple,*
> *The purple was all covered with orfrays,*
> *And it had pictured in orfrays,*
> *Histories of dukes and kings.*

She had, in addition, a girdle, extremely costly, set with precious stones with magical qualities. Round her neck was a collar of gold, likewise set with jewels.

This matter of a collar or necklace seems to have been of great importance. Margaret Paston, writing to her husband in 1453, tells him that Queen Margaret of Anjou had been visiting Norwich and the writer had had to borrow her cousin Elizabeth's device 'for I durst not for shame go with my beads among so many fresh gentlewomen. I pray you,' she begs, 'do your cost on me against Whitsuntide that I may have something for my neck.' How effectually does such a feminine *cri de cœur* bridge the gap between the medieval centuries and our own!

5

PILGRIMS AND CRUSADERS

Right worshipful husband, I recommend me to you,
desiring to hear of your welfare, thanking God of the
amending of the great disease that you have had.
My mother promised another image of wax of the
weight of you to Our Lady of Walsingham . . . and I
have promised to go on pilgrimage to Walsingham
and to St Leonard's Priory for you. I pray you, send
me word as hastily as you may, how your sore
doeth. . . .

'TO go on pilgrimage.' This, to Margaret Paston, was
the greatest contribution she could make towards the
healing of her husband's 'great disease'. When the
highest qualified doctors available had done their best
for a patient, when sorcerers, 'quacks' and 'women
pretenders' had used their spells and revolting concoc-
tions with little or no avail, there still remained what,
to the medieval mind, was one of the most powerful
sources of help for the cure of illness—a pilgrimage to
some famous shrine of the Virgin, such as Walsingham,
or to that of a martyr, saint or holy bishop. For this
desire to visit sacred shrines was widespread and deeply
implanted in the nature of medieval men and women.
The reasons for this were as varied as the character of
the pilgrims themselves. For some, such a journey held
out the hope of pardon for sin, the assurance of deliver-
ance from damnation after death, or at least the lessen-

ing of the term of penance for misdeeds. To others, it was a way of escape from days of boredom when nothing exciting ever happened. To the serf or criminal, to go on pilgrimage could bring freedom from servitude and imprisonment. But to many devout Christians, the desire to worship Christ in Jerusalem, in the very place where the 'Gospel had shone forth from the Cross', was an overriding emotion which enabled them to endure the acute discomfort and dangers of a medieval journey or sea-voyage, to face sudden death from avalanche, starvation or murder *en route*, or to risk capture by pirates or Moslems, with the horrors of slavery to follow.

From as early as the fourth century Christians had been journeying as pilgrims to Rome and Jerusalem, and during the eleventh, Cluniac monks had made the shrine of St James at Compostella equally famous. The overland route was made attractive by monasteries and hostels in the towns along the way. At Tours, Vézelay (*44*), Le Puy, Arles, St Gilles, St Pierre de Moissac and St Jean d'Angly, shelter and food was provided for pilgrims and horses. At Roncesvalles, in addition, were hospices for the sick, with beds and baths and a fare which included almonds, pomegranates and other luscious fruit. Those who took the sea route, however, often had cause to regret their choice. Ships (*47*) carrying 60–100 pilgrims, crammed together so that they could scarcely move, often provided neither shelter nor food for their passengers. One of these pilgrims has described—not without humour—the trials of such a voyage in the fifteenth century. We hear the captain shouting his orders to the cook, 'Make ready anon our meat', then, roaring with laughter as he looks down at his pallid-faced human cargo, he bawls, 'Our pilgrims have no lust to eat. I pray God give them rest.'

Accounts of the overland journey to Rome from England have been left by several fifteenth-century pilgrims and travellers, including that of William Wey, a Fellow of Eton, who journeyed through Flanders and 'Duchelond' (Germany) by way of Antwerp, Coblenz, Worms, Ulm, Memingen, through the Alps into Lombardy, on to Verona, Bologna, Siena, Viterbo and so to Rome. On a second visit he was obliged to leave his direct route in order to avoid the conflict raging between two bishops on the Rhine, and to bypass the lands of the Duke of Austria whose estates then lay under an interdict. But these were minor difficulties. More perilous was the crossing of the Alps. A Spanish pilgrim, Pero Tafur, journeying from south to north has described his passage through the St Gothard Pass in 1437:

The third day after leaving Milan I arrived at a German town where all my animals and baggage were loaded upon boats which then crossed a great lake which receives its waters from the Alps. . . . The next day I departed and arrived at the foot of the St Gothard Pass, high up in the Alps. The day following, after the necessary preparations were completed, we began the ascent. It was now the end of August and the snow was melting in the heat, making the crossing extremely perilous. The people in those parts use oxen which are used to the track. One of these goes ahead dragging by a long rope a trailer which resembles a Castilian threshing machine. The passenger sits on this while his horse, held by a guiding rein, follows behind. If any accident happens, only the ox is involved. Before entering the narrow defiles firearms are discharged to bring down any loose snow from above, for such avalanches sometimes bury travellers. . . . The mountains are

44   The nave of the great Romanesque abbey church of La Madeleine,
Vézelay, built between 1104–32

45   The Crusader castle of Krak des Chevaliers, Syria, was built by the
     Knights Hospitaller early in the twelfth century

46   Pilgrims setting out from Canterbury
     English manuscript illumination

thickly populated, inns and small hamlets are numerous.

On reaching the hermitage of St Gothard, Tafur paid off the hired oxen and took the road to Basle through the mountains. Adam of Usk, who passed through the St Gothard Pass in 1402, was also drawn in an ox-wagon 'half dead with cold, while his eyes were blindfolded so that he could not see the dangers of the pass'.

The journey to Jerusalem, however, held the greatest dangers. It was usual to sail from Venice where pilgrim boats left for the Holy Land in May. William Wey, who made the voyage twice, has left what he called a 'prevysoun', or list of directions, for prospective pilgrims to Jerusalem:

> Be sure if you go in a galley to choose a place on the upper stage, for in the lowest it is right smouldering hot and stinking. And you shall pay for your galley and for your meat and drink to Jaffa, and back again to Venice, 49 ducats to be in a good, honest place, where you will be comfortable and properly looked after. But take care to make your covenant with your patron before the duke and other lords of Venice, under surety of 100 ducats. This includes stopping at certain harbours on the way to get fresh water, bread and meat.

Before going on board the galley William directed that the traveller should buy a bed, a mattress, two pillows and two pairs of sheets and one quilt from a man in St Mark's Square. 'And you shall pay for these four ducats and on returning sell the same back to their former owner for one and a half ducats, though the goods be broken and worn.' A bargain should also be made with the patron to have hot meat served twice daily with good wine and fresh water, 'and, if ye may come thereto, also biscuits'. Two barrels of wine and one of fresh water for the traveller's use should be taken aboard. 'Also buy a chest to put your things in.' The 'things' included a supply of bread, cheese, eggs, fruit, bacon and wine, 'for some time you shall have feeble bread, wine and stinking water, so that many times you will be glad to eat of your own'. William goes on to advise that confections, laxatives, restoratives, ginger, rice, figs, raisins, pepper, saffron, cloves, mace, as well as a little cauldron, frying pan, dishes, platters, wooden saucers, glass cups, and a grater for bread shall also be stored in the chest. When he ends by recommending the installation of a cage with half-a-dozen live hens in it, with half a bushel of meal seed for their food on the already overcrowded upper deck, it becomes a puzzle to know where other pilgrims stowed themselves and their belongings.

William's advice on arriving at ports of call is anything but Christian in character:

> When you come to haven towns, if you shall tarry there three days, go betimes to land to secure lodging ahead of the others, for it will be taken quickly, and, if there is any good food, get it before the others arrive. On arriving at Jaffa, the port for Jerusalem, the same haste must be observed so as to secure one of the best asses. You shall pay no more for the best than for the worst.

It seems clear that he had been robbed on his previous visit to the Holy Land. 'Take good heed of your knives and other small things,' he warns, 'for the Saracens will talk with you and make you good cheer, but they will steal from you what you have if they can.'

Pero Tafur gives more details of the arrival at Jaffa than we find in Wey's account. He says that the ship's arrival is known almost at once to the Prior of Mount Sion, who sends two of his friars to the Governor of Jerusalem who return with the Sultan's safe conduct. The pilgrims then go ashore and deliver their names in writing for the Governor's use while the friars retain one for themselves.

We know from other accounts that most pilgrims had to await the arrival of the safe conduct—which was often delayed—in a row of caves on the seashore, known as St Peter's, where the filth was indescribable. When at last the matter of tribute was arranged, they were allowed to set off for Jerusalem on asses.

William also provides a list of Greek words and phrases useful for the pilgrim. 'Good morrow', and 'Welcome', 'Tell me the way', and 'Woman, have you good wine?' and, most important of all, 'How much?' and 'Too much'. Indeed, one of the results of pilgrimages was to increase the knowledge of the French language since during the later Middle Ages, French, not Latin, had become the language used for conversation by the educated classes. Sir John Mandeville, at the beginning of the fifteenth century tells us, concerning his tales of travel:

And know that I would have put this little book into Latin for brevity, but, because many understand Romance better . . . and that lords, knights and other noblemen who do not understand Latin, or but little, and have been beyond the seas may know whether I speak truth or not.

In the fourteenth century many conversation manuals were written to help travellers 'to speak, to pronounce well and to write correctly sweet French which is the finest and most graceful language, the noblest to speak of any, in the world, after the Latin of the schools'.

Among the many sacred shrines to be visited in Jerusalem, the Church of the Holy Sepulchre was especially revered, as the last earthly resting-place of Our Lord. It was, however, only opened twice a year, from Good Friday to Easter Monday and from the Vigil of the Holy Cross until the Vespers following (13 and 14 September). Its guardians remained locked in until the arrival of the next season's pilgrims. Food was handed to them through holes in the door.

Today, Christians are admitted to the Mohammedan Mosque of Omar, but, although Tafur visited it in 1437, it was at the risk of his life:

That night I bargained with a renegade, a native of Portugal, and offered him two ducats if he would get me into the Temple of Solomon, and he consented. At one o'clock in the night I entered, dressed in his clothes, and saw the Temple which is a single nave, the whole ornamented with mosaic work. The floor and walls are of the most beautiful white stone, and the place is hung with so many lamps that they all seem to be joined together. The roof above is quite flat and covered with lead. They say when Solomon built it, it was the most magnificent building in the whole world . . . without doubt, it is still unmatched. If I had been recognised there I should have been killed immediately. . . . The renegade who had escorted me now returned with me to Mount Sion where the friars mourned me as one already dead, since I had not come again at the appointed time and they rejoiced greatly to see me again as did also the gentlemen of my company.

An earlier pilgrim than Tafur to Jerusalem was Richard, Abbot of St Vannes, who went there with a great company in 1026. He was one of those whose deep faith had made him ardently long to visit the Holy

City. On arriving at last at the sacred place where he had so wished to be, we are told that his tears over-flowed:

> When he gazed on the Pillar of Pilate in the Praeto-rium and relived the binding and the scourging of the Saviour, the spitting, the smiting, the mocking, the crown of thorns; when, standing on Calvary, he beheld in his mind the Saviour crucified, pierced with a lance, mocked by the passers-by, crying out with a loud voice and surrendering His spirit, when he, Richard, relived these scenes, what heartfelt pain, what bitterness of tears do you think sprang from the pangs of such remembrance?

Two centuries later, in 1395, another pilgrim, the Lord of Anglure, with a troop of French pilgrims set out for the Holy Land. In Venice, 'a most excellent, noble and fine town, all seated in the sea', they visited the wonderful relics which the city possessed: the arm of St George, the roasted flesh of St Lawrence 'albeit turned to powder', the staff of St Nicholas, the ear of St Paul and one of the jars of Cana in which Our Lord had turned water into wine. Perhaps most marvellous of all was the tooth of Goliath whom David slew. This

47   Pilgrim ships

48   On pilgrimage

molar, 'know you, is more than half a foot long and weighs 12 pounds'. A tooth truly worthy of such a giant! Such a sight, described to townsfolk and villagers at home, would be enough to set them all agog to go on pilgrimage. Indeed, the Lord of Anglure and his party had probably been attracted by the adventure of the journey, almost as much as by the rewards of piety to be gained in visiting the Holy City. A mere threat of shipwreck was not enough to damp their exuberance, for on their way home, overtaken by a fearful storm, they had to put into a port of Cyprus for shelter. The welcome given them by the king more than compensated for all they had suffered. Royal carts arrived at the ship, laden with provisions—100 poultry, 20 sheep, 2 oxen, wine in plenty and the whitest of bread. After they had feasted they were bidden to the court, where the king and queen with their children received them—'for to entertain pilgrims was to entertain the Christ'. Next day, the king, a great huntsman, invited the male pilgrims to join him in the chase.

As the Lord of Anglure ends the account of his many adventures, we experience his sense of achievement, and, even more, the relief and contentment of the traveller, safe at home once more after arduous journeys: 'On Thursday, the 22nd day of June, the day before the eve of the feast of St John the Baptist, in the year of grace of Our Lord, 1396, we found ourselves again dining in Anglure.'

Yet, although Jerusalem was, without doubt, unrivalled as a pilgrim city, each shrine held its own attractions, sold its own particular badges, told its own tale of miracles and cures, and dispensed its own spiritual awards. At Rocamadour in France, one of the famous pilgrim centres, the right to sell leaden images of Our Lady had been granted to a local family—the de Valons—in return for military services. They shared their profits with the Bishop of Tulle. But, in 1425, the poverty of the surrounding country was so extreme that for two years the bishop handed over his income from the sale of badges to buy food for his starving flock. Louis XI, a veteran pilgrim, had his cap adorned with lead images and badges—his only decorations.

This wearing of badges was later to be derided by Erasmus. 'I pray you, what array is this that I see you in?' he puts into the mouth of one of his characters. 'Methinks your clothing is of cockle shells. On every side you are weighed down with brooches of lead and tin. How prettily garnished you are with straw coronets, and how full are your arms with snakes' eggs.'

At Rocamadour, also, the famous sword, Durandal, which had belonged to Roland, was treasured. It was from this town that he set out on his ill-fated expedition to Spain against the Moors. Here, too, besides relics of the saints, votive offerings brought by the faithful were found in abundance. Jewels, rich vestments, gold and silver ornaments had been deposited over the years to win the favour of heaven for their donors. Numerous tresses of women's hair were reminders of the story long associated with the shrine. A woman pilgrim, famed for her beauty, had, through loose living, become blind. On the way to Rocamadour she prayed to the Virgin that her sight might be restored. This was granted but, on her arrival, she was not allowed to enter the shrine. While she was confessing her sins outside to a priest he, looking at her fair face, said, 'Dear friend, I fear that these lovely tresses of yours have done great hurt to those who have gazed at them. Offer them now in honour of God and Our Lady.' The tresses were cut, and carried into the church on a pole and there placed with others, similarly surrendered. The lady followed, to give thanks to the Virgin for her salvation. But, on the homeward journey, like Lot's wife, the shorn beauty looked regretfully back, bemoaning the loss of her hair and wishing she had it again. Her wish was immediately granted, but with her hair her blindness also returned.

Many shrines of the Blessed Virgin seem to have been associated with miracles, and innumerable stories of her wonder-working powers were told throughout the Middle Ages. One concerns a Flemish monk, who was painting a picture of heaven and hell on the portals of his abbey. He was engaged in portraying the Devil as hideously as possible when His Satanic Majesty, appearing in person, begged the monk to paint him as a young and handsome man. The monk refused and the angry Devil pulled away the scaffold on which the artist was working. But, as the monk fell a statue of the Virgin, in a niche below the portal, stretched out her arms and held him in safety until help arrived.

In the number of its chapels and churches which contained prized relics, Rome was especially rich. One of the most highly venerated was the Holy Vernicle. This was the napkin on which an imprint of Christ's face appeared after St Veronica had wiped the sweat from his brow on the way to Calvary. The mere sight of the Vernicle earned for the pilgrim a 12,000 years' indulgence—for the citizen of Rome this was reduced to a mere 3,000 years! In a fourteenth-century poem, *The Stations of the Cross*, the author asks, why go to Jerusalem or to St Catherine's monastery on Mount Sinai to gain indulgence when the 157 chapels and the 1,005 churches in Rome are so generous in granting this? To

49　Stealing drink from a blind beggar

mount the 29 steps leading to the chapel where St Peter
sang his first Mass:

> *As often as you will thither come,*
> *Seven thousand year you get pardon.*

In the chapel where the bones of 10,000 martyrs were
lying we are told that by singing there a Mass for a
friend, release from hell would be gained for him,
while a visit to the pillar on which Christ was bound,
the sight of St Thomas' cloak or of St Blaise's arm, a
glimpse of a piece of the True Cross or of St Martin's
well—or indeed, of any of the other innumerable relics
to be found in Rome—would bring to pilgrims indulgences for thousands of years. These indulgences were
remissions of the punishment still due to sin after
sacramental absolution; they did not remit either the
guilt or eternal punishment for sin.

Naturally, impostors and charlatans abounded to
take advantage of the many earthly benefits accorded
to genuine pilgrims. These 'professionals' made an easy
living, begging their way from shrine to shrine, and
enjoying the free entertainment provided in monasteries and hospices. Each had his scrip and burdon, that
is the wallet for food and the staff, with an iron point at
one end and a knob at the other, carried by all pilgrims.

But, more important, his hooded gown would be
covered with badges and brooches to prove he had
visited the various shrines—shells from St James of
Compostella, the head of John the Baptist from Amiens,
a holy napkin from Rome, heads of the Three Kings
from Cologne, an image of the Virgin from Rocamadour, and in his hand a palm branch, sign of the pilgrim
who had visited Jerusalem. Aided by a vivid imagination and agile tongue, these rogues poured out lurid
stories of the wonders seen on their travels, their well-
filled scrips witnessing to the delight, gullibility or
simple faith of their hearers. But by all governments
these false pilgrims were regarded with disfavour. An
ordinance of Charles VI of France forbade pilgrimages
to Rome, and other countries made similar laws. These
were aimed at the professional vagabond, who, unless
he could produce a sealed licence from the king giving
him leave to go on pilgrimage, would find himself in
prison.

Dislike of these professional beggars, as well as a
growing feeling of anti-clericalism in the later Middle
Ages, led to criticism of pilgrimages themselves. *The
Romance of Reynard*, a French poem, satirises the desire
of pilgrims to go to Rome. Reynard, seeking absolution
for his sins, goes to a hermit to confess. The holy man
advises him to seek absolution from the Pope in Rome.
So Reynard equips himself with wallet and staff, and,
well pleased that he looks as a pilgrim should—his
scrip fits his neck quite perfectly—he sets off. Soon he
meets Belin the Sheep and a donkey eating thistles in a
ditch, who turns out to be Bernart the archpriest. He
persuades them both to accompany him. But, as night is
falling, they seek shelter at a house whose owners appear
to be away. Finding salted meat, cheese and ale in the
buttery, they proceed to have supper. After drinking
rather too well, they grow merry and begin to sing—

Belin baa-ing, Bernart braying and Reynard howling in a high falsetto. Now the house belonged to Primant the Wolf. His relatives, hearing the hullabaloo, come and attack the pilgrims who do not escape without injury. Reynard then calls a conference. 'My lords,' he groans, 'by my head, this wandering is loathsome. Many a good man there is who has never seen Rome. Others return from the seven saints even worse than before. I have decided to go home, to live by honest labour and be charitable to the poor.' The others heartily agreed, and all three returned to their own homes once more.

This desire for a quiet life contrasted with the spirit which had pervaded Europe during the eleventh and twelfth centuries. Expansion and development were the hall-mark of this period, reflected in agriculture, in population, in religious ardour and reform, in the unprecedented increase of monasteries, in the growth of towns, in military techniques. In the intellectual, scientific and social spheres, on every front of medieval life, there was activity and growth. Another outlet for all this accumulating energy was the Crusades. While it is true that the cruelties and intolerance of the fierce Seljuk Turks who, in the eleventh century had captured Jerusalem, together with the appeal of the Emperor Alexius of Constantinople for military help from the West, were instrumental in bringing about the actual outbreak of hostilities, yet the stage had long been set for the conflict. For the Crusades were but another facet of European expansion which had already begun and which was to continue throughout the succeeding century.

When, consequently, in 1095 Pope Urban II preached the First Crusade at Clermont, he met with a wide and enthusiastic response. The Holy Wars held a universal appeal. Nevertheless, they were in direct

opposition to the monastic spirit of a St Anselm who,
as early as 1086, had no doubts upon the true character
of 'religious' wars. Replying to a young man who asked
his advice as to whether he should become a monk, or
join the army in defence of the tottering empire of
Constantinople, Anselm wrote:

> I advise you, I counsel you, I pray and beseech you,
> as one who is dear to me, to abandon that Jerusalem
> which is now not a vision of peace, but of tribulation,
> to leave aside the treasures of Constantinople and
> Babylon, which are to be seized on with hands soaked
> in blood, and to set out on the road to the heavenly
> Jerusalem which is a vision of peace, where you will
> find treasures which only those who despise these
> [earthly] ones can receive.

This advice Pope Urban II would certainly have
deplored when, 11 years later, he preached his recruit-
ment sermon at Clermont. Urging the knights and
landowners who had filled Europe with carnage and
bloodshed during their internal wars to 'cease from
contending against their brethren and relatives, to
cease from living the life of robbers and to become
instead the soldiers of Christ', he then pointed out how
closely Europe was hemmed in on every side by infidels.
'Asia, too, the source of Christianity, where all but two
of the Apostles had met their deaths, is held by
Moslems.' There, small pockets of Christians 'look to us
with silent longing for the liberty they have lost'. As for
Africa, where once lived the brightest spirits of
Christendom, she had been lost to Moslems for over
200 years. Even Europe itself was not wholly Christian,
for

> who will give the name of Christian to those bar-
> barians who live in remote islands and seek their

living on the icy ocean as if they were whales? This little portion of the world that is ours is pressed upon by Turks and Saracens, who for 300 years have held Spain and the Balearic Islands and who now live in hope of devouring the rest.

A terrifying picture, which must have startled many of his hearers out of their complacence! For since 732, when Charles Martel had defeated the Moslems at Poitiers in France and driven them back into Spain, men had come to think of the Pyrenees as a boundary beyond which their enemies would never again venture. On the east, Constantinople had seemed an impregnable bulwark against the infidels. Yet the Turks had but recently, in 1071, won a resounding victory in Asia, at Manzikert, and the emperor even more recently had sent an appeal to the West for military aid.

Fear, religious zeal to free the holy places from the domination of the Turk, desire for adventure, the hope of gain, either spiritual or material—all played their part in bringing an enthusiastic response to the Pope's harangue. In addition, through his eloquence all the fervour that had been glowing at the heart of Christendom throughout the previous hundred years, was liberated, as a banked-down bonfire, suddenly stirred,

50   Saladin being unhorsed

bursts into violent flame. With a great shout his
listeners surged forward. 'God wills it! God wills it!'
they cried and, through the months that followed,
knights and peasants, workmen, vagabonds and criminals, even the aged and infirm, women and children,
hastened in their thousands to receive the future badge
of all Crusaders—the red cross. This they 'straightway
began to sew on the right shoulders of their garments
crying that they would all follow in the footsteps of
Christ.' From every nation, also, men speaking
unknown tongues landed in France. Even from faraway
Scotland a contingent arrived, 'drawn from their
native swamps, with their bare legs, rough cloaks,
purses hanging from their shoulders, hung about with
arms, ridiculous enough in our eyes, but offering the aid
of their faith and devotion to our cause'.

It was a motley, badly armed and undisciplined
host, under the direction of Peter the Hermit and a
dozen or more knights, that set out for Constantinople.

51   Crusaders besieging Antioch

The main army followed later. As this first ragged array straggled across Europe, in most districts they were kindly received, but from time to time serious trouble arose owing to the violence and turbulence of many of the Crusaders. Not only did they steal and pillage *en route*, set fire to mills and other property, but even sacked Belgrade itself, afterwards burning the town from which its inhabitants had fled in terror. In Constantinople their approach was awaited with consternation, if not dismay. Anna Comnena, the Emperor Alexius' daughter, has set down her own reactions as the 'People's Crusade' drew near to the most wealthy and cultured city of Europe. It seemed to her the 'whole of the West, with all the barbarians that live between the farther side of the Adriatic and the Pillars of Hercules, had migrated in a body, and were marching into Asia through intervening Europe, making the journey with all their household.' These unwelcome arrivals, although Alexius received them with kindness and courtesy, were later ferried across the Bosphorus to Asia where they were finally massacred by the Turks.

The better-organised armies of knights, after many vicissitudes, reached the Holy Land. Aided mainly by dissensions amongst the Moslems, they succeeded in capturing Antioch and Jerusalem, where a Christian kingdom and princedom were established. The difficulties and sufferings of these first Crusaders are described for us by an eye-witness:

We pursued those abominable Turks through a land which was deserted, waterless and uninhabitable, from which we barely emerged or escaped alive. We suffered greatly from hunger and thirst and found nothing to eat except prickly plants. On such food we survived, wretchedly enough, but we lost most of our horses, so that many of our knights had to go as foot soldiers. We also had to use oxen as mounts and were compelled to use goats, sheep and dogs as beasts of burden.

Between the eleventh and thirteenth centuries, nine Crusades were fought. Their aim had been to save eastern Christendom from the Moslems, yet when they ended it was wholly under Mohammedan rule. Nor can it be claimed that the Crusades, nor the way of life established in the kingdoms they created, brought about any changes in western Europe that had not already begun or that would not have been brought about without these protracted and wasteful wars. The pointed arch, some development in military architecture, and the introduction of heraldry to the West, may be ascribed to the Crusades. No doubt, also, pilgrims and soldiers, returning to Europe after witnessing the luxurious way of life followed by the Crusaders who settled in Outremer, brought back a desire for similar comforts and embellishments in their own homes. But the flow of luxuries from East to West had already started before the Crusades began. By the eleventh century, but probably earlier, silk weavers from Constantinople had been established in Cyprus and Greece and were producing exquisite textiles, mainly silk, and by the twelfth century Sicily had become the centre of a flourishing weaving industry which was supplying both Christian and Moslems with their wares. One of their favourtie motifs was the eagle. These stuffs were found most often as hangings in secular buildings, but they were also used in churches and for costumes both ecclesiastical and lay.

It is true that Venice and the Italian cities owed much of their rapid development and their consequent wealth to the partition of the Eastern Empire after the destruction of Constantinople in 1204 by the Fourth Crusade. But the price paid for this was disastrous. True too, many Byzantine scholars found a home in Italy with a consequent spread of humanism in the West. But again it was tragic that this should have been gained by the ruin of eastern Christendom.

It is also a fact that Byzantine art survived and achieved a splendid

52   Design from a Byzantine textile

flowering in the fourteenth and early fifteenth centuries, but the bastion of Europe against the Turks had been undermined by those very men who should have strengthened it. The gateway which the Crusaders should have defended was, by their cupidity and greed (especially that of Venice and its wily Doge) and by their lack of understanding of a different culture, so weakened that it finally fell, to admit into the very heart of Europe an infidel and alien civilisation. The betrayal of 1204 by the Crusaders was to result in untold suffering, in persecution and slavery for the Christian peoples of the Balkans.

One social change in western Europe was probably hastened, though not entirely caused, by the Crusades —the lessening of the feudal power of kings and magnates. No doubt, however, the ever-growing volume of trade, and the increasing power of the towns would have accomplished this eventually, if more slowly. Nevertheless, in order to raise money to equip them-

53   The capture of Richard Coeur
de Lion

selves and pay for horses, arms and retainers, crusading kings and magnates sold many charters of freedom 'which unlocked the fetters of the slave, secured the farm of the peasant and the shop of the artificer and gradually restored substance and a soul to the most useful and numerous part of the community'.

A final and perhaps somewhat imperceptible result of the Crusades was the broadening of men's minds in the West by contact with the East. Richard Coeur de Lion and the Moslem leader Saladin have become symbols not only of the chivalrous knight, but of the understanding that was possible between men of alien faith and culture. Indeed many of the Moslems and Franks who lived side by side in the Holy Land—or Outremer, as it was called—reached a high degree of respect, toleration and even friendship for each other. Ousama, a friend of Saladin, who wrote an entertaining chronicle about the Crusades, has a story which illustrates this camaraderie. He tells us that a certain Frankish knight had given him permission to pray in a little chapel in what had formerly been a Moslem mosque, but had become a Christian church. Another Frank, seeing Ousama at prayer, threw him out of the building. The Moslem returned to pray and was again thrown out. But his Frankish friend, seeing the second ejection, went to Ousama's aid. 'He is one of the Franks but newly come to Outremer', the knight explained. 'He does not understand the ways of those of us who have lived out here for so long.'

Such an attitude towards the great enemies of

Christendom was not, of course, common in western Europe and, no doubt, would have been looked upon with distrust by the great majority. Nevertheless it is an indication of a broadening of outlook, of a breaking of barriers and an enlargement of vision to which pilgrimages, the Crusades and trading ventures all contributed their quota.

6

MONKS AND FRIARS

MONASTERIES and priories! The words conjure up
the magnificent ruins of, perhaps, Fountains or of
Rievaulx Abbey in England. Or maybe the fortress-like
outlines of Monte Cassino in Italy, or of the monastery
of St Gall in Switzerland on its mountain perch? Yet
such impressive and splendid surroundings, indicative
of wealth and wide acres, were not where the earliest
Christian monks were to be found. For the word
'monk' (from the Greek *monos*) is, properly speaking, a
man by himself, and it was in a wattle hut in the desert,
in some cave of the mountains or merely beneath the
woven branches of forest trees, that the earliest anchor-
ites made their home. Here, living alone, they existed
on berries, nuts or a handful of dates—for it was in the
East that monasticism first took root. By living a life of
prayer, contemplation and extreme asceticism they
sought to subdue the natural man, and the natural
man's craving for the pleasures of earthly life, that they
might attain the greater joys of heaven. For their first
aim was the salvation of their own souls. Yet, in spite of
themselves they affected others. Soon they were joined
by men and women who, living in separate cells near by,
sought to follow their example. After a time it became
necessary for sets of rules to be drawn up to regulate the
lives of these monks. One of the earliest of these was the
Rule of St Basil of Pontus (*d.* 379) and it was used

throughout the Byzantine Empire at least as late as the eighth and ninth centuries.

By the beginning of the fifth century, however, many monasteries had been established in the West. Those of St Cassian at Marseilles and of St Honorat in the Île de Lérins, in the south of France, were especially famous. Cassian, who had visited monasteries in the East, drew up a rule for his monks which was widely followed in the West. To attain purity of heart was one of the chief aims of his teaching. To do this 'we must seek solitude and submit to fastings, vigils, toils, bodily nakedness, reading and other virtues'.

By 530, Caesarius of Arles, a monk of Lérins, had also organised a monastery under a rule, and even earlier monasteries based on eastern rules had been established in Ireland. By the sixth century these were so famed for their learning that scholars were going there by the old trade routes—from the Loire to Cork in three days. In 550 a shipload of 50 landed there; others sailed up the Irish Sea to Bangor. Bede gives us a glimpse of Ireland in 664. In that year English nobles had fled there from the plague.

> Some of them dedicated themselves to the monastic life, others rejoiced to give themselves to learning, going from one master to the other. All these, the Irish willingly received and supplied them with daily food, with books for study and with teaching all free of charge.

By 700 culture and learning were having a desperate struggle to survive on the Continent. But on the isles and loughs of Ireland monasteries still carried on their peaceful and ordered life. To this secure shelter scholars fled from Gaul, driven like seeds before the blast, and like fruitful seeds they were later to bring forth an hundredfold in a barbaric and devastated Europe. For

the dreaded beak-prowed longships came at last to the
loughs and rivers. From 795 onwards the Norse
ravaged the once peaceful monasteries. An Irish monk
writing in his cell on a bitter night of storm welcomed
the harsh weather:

> *Bitter is the wind tonight, it tosses the ocean's white hair,*
> *I need not fear—as on a night of calm sea—the fierce raiders*
> *from Lochlann.*

But at last the raids became so destructive that the
monks had to flee. Looking fearfully back, they groaned
to see the sky above their loved monastery blood-red
and flame-lit. Then many an Irishman ended his days
in a Continental abbey, longing for the grey skies and
green fields of his homeland:

> *In all my wanderings round this world of care,*
> *In all my griefs—and God has given my share—*
> *I still had hopes my latest hour to crown,*
> *Among those humble bowers to lay me down;*
> *And as a hare whom horns and hounds pursue,*
> *Points to that place from which at first she flew,*
> *I still had hopes, my long vexations past,*
> *There to return and die at home at last.*

Yet Ireland's loss was Europe's gain. The Abbot of
Aghaboe went to Salzburg and became its bishop;
Dubthach who copied out a book of Priscian's grammar
at Leiden finished, we know from the gloss or note
written in the margin, 'at three o'clock of an April
afternoon in A.D. 838'. Cairbre of Inch-madoc and
Mahee of Nendrum have left manuscripts written in
the *scriptorium* of St Gall. One Irish monk as far from
home as Reichenau on Lake Constance reveals his
humour, learning and love for his little white cat in the
poem he wrote there. As we read, both he and Pangur

54   Beggars being given relief
Miniature from an English manuscript

55   A meeting between the two great saints, Francis and Dominic
*Fifteenth-century terracotta relief by Andrea della Robbia from the Loggia di
San Paolo, Florence*

56   Henry I dreams that the English peasants will rise against him

57   The King also dreams the clergy turn against him
Both miniatures from the twelfth-century English 'Chronicle of John of Worcester'

Ban seem to be in the room with us, not in their monkish
call viewed down the long vista of eleven centuries:

> *I and Pangur Ban my cat*
> *'Tis a like task we are .at,*
> *Hunting mice is his delight,*
> *Hunting words I sit all night.*
>
> *'Tis a merry thing to see,*
> *At our tasks how glad are we*
> *When at home we sit and find,*
> *Entertainment to our mind.*
>
> *'Gainst the wall he sets his eye,*
> *Full and fierce and sharp and sly,*
> *'Gainst the wall of knowledge, I*
> *All my little wisdom try.*
>
> *So in peace our task we ply:*
> *Pangur Ban my cat, and I*
> *In our arts we find our bliss,*
> *I have mine and he has his.*

Ireland indeed played a many-sided role in the
building of the medieval civilisation which was beginning to emerge like a phoenix from the ashes of the
classical world. In 690 Willibrord, a Northumbrian
who had studied in Ireland, converted the Frisians and
founded the monastery of Echternach in present-day
Luxembourg. The beauty and style of the Echternach
Gospels bear witness not only to the missionary's
labours, but also to his work in helping to diffuse
Northumbrian and Irish art through Europe.

Many of the monasteries which have played an
influential role in European history were of Irish
foundation. St Martin's of Cologne and St Peter's of
Ratisbon were Irish in origin; Warzburg, Nuremberg,
Salzburg, Eichstadt, Vienna and Prague were centres

58   St Benedict giving his Rule to monks

of Irish-Christian influence; while Columban founded Luxeuil and Bobbio in Italy in 609, his disciple gave his name to the monastery of St Gall. St Bertin, Jumièges, St Riquier and Remiremont, Corbie and Reichenau do not exhaust the list. Some of these nurtured the greatest scholars of the Middle Ages and Columban did much to reform the Merovingian Church. True the Rule that he drew up—'Let not a man seek his bed until he is already asleep on his feet' is one tenet—proved too hard for most monks. They preferred the kindlier Rule of St Benedict. Yet the austere Irish master loved both animals and flowers. He was usually to be seen with a squirrel on his shoulder, and once, when the gardener at his monastery at Luxeuil interrupted him at his teaching, bringing a scent of roses with him into the room, Columban cried out, 'Ah, beloved! 'Tis thou should be lord of this monastery.'

Actually there was much in common between the ideals of St Columban and those of the earlier St Benedict. Both believed it was better for monks to live in communities rather than as hermits. St Benedict's Rule (526) was a compilation drawn from Cassian, from the Lives of the Desert Fathers and from St Augustine. It also contains matter found in the 'Rule of the Master' drawn up by an unknown monk. Nevertheless, Benedict's Rule bears the imprint of his own genius for organisation, of his outstanding personality and of his balance and moderation. It was this rule on which Latin monasticism is based; indeed it has been justly called the most important document of the Middle Ages.

The sort of community which St Benedict envisaged had as its keystone an Abbot who was pre-eminently the father of his flock, not chosen for his own advancement, or for the satisfaction of ruling, but a man who desired to be loved rather than feared. Nevertheless he was to be given implicit obedience, although all important business was to be discussed by the whole community of monks: 'The brothers shall give their advice in all humility and deference. They shall not presume to discuss their views heatedly.' The final decision lay with the abbot: 'Once he has decided let all obey him.'

How difficult it could be in practice to work according to this rule can be gathered from the experience of an English abbot. Although living at a later date—in the twelfth century—similar problems must constantly have cropped up throughout the ages. It happened in Abbot Samson's monastery at Bury St Edmunds that the cellarer of the abbey, who was responsible for supplying it with food and drink, had asked that the annual allowance of £50 should be paid to him as a lump sum instead of by monthly instalments. Reluctantly, Abbot Samson granted his request. Within a short time the cellarer was overspent to the tune of £26 and 'was like to owe 50 before Michaelmas'. On hearing this the abbot 'took it very ill' and complained in Chapter:

There is neither clerk nor monk that dare tell me the cause of the debt. It is said that it is to be found in the immoderate feasting that takes place in the prior's lodging, with the assent of the prior and cellarer, and

in superfluous extravagance in the guest-house, due
to the carelessness of the guest-master. 'You see,'
he said, 'the great debt that weighs upon us. Tell me
how the matter may be set right.'

Many cloister monks smiled at this, and were
pleased at what had been said, saying the abbot's
words were true. The prior put the blame on the
cellarer, the cellarer on the guest-master. Everybody
excused himself. We did, indeed, know the truth,
but we were silent because we were afraid. On the
morrow the abbot came again and spoke to the
convent. 'Give your advice as to how your cellary
may be better managed.' Nobody replied, save one,
who said there was certainly no superfluity in the
refectory which could account for the debt. On the
third day the abbot said the same; and one replied,
'The advice should proceed from you as being our
head.'

The Abbot made answer, 'Since you will not give
your advice, and do not know how to govern your
house, the management of the monastery falls upon
me, as your father and supreme guardian. I take into
my hand your cellary and all expenses in respect of
guests, and the management of all things both within
and without.' This said, he deposed the cellarer and
guest-master and set in their places two other monks,
and set over them a clerk from his own table. There
was division of opinion over this high-handed
action, but Abbot Samson was a strong man and
desiring to have his house well-disciplined wisely
ignored the murmuring, and proceeded on his way
unmoved.

St Benedict's Rule also made provision for the ordering of the monk's day. This began at sunrise with the
service of Prime, actually the second of the seven

offices. After it, the brothers went to wash in basins or troughs in the cloisters, before breaking their fast— unless it was a fast day or Lent. Then Terce and Mass was celebrated, followed by a meeting in the chapter-house to discuss business, hear complaints and for the abbot to receive novices on occasions. Afterwards the monks followed their allotted pursuits, some did farm or garden work, others instructed the novices or copied and illuminated manuscripts. As the wealth and property of the monasteries increased offices were allocated to different monks to deal with it—the cellarer was in charge of buying in food and drink, the guest-master managed everything that concerned the guest-house, the novice-master ran the school for oblates or those intending to become monks, and the librarian supervised the lending out, as well as the copying, of manuscripts. Sext, the fourth service of the day, was followed by High Mass which became more and more elaborate. Then came dinner in the frater during which one monk read from the refectory pulpit. Five hours work followed Nones which was succeeded by a short rest before Vespers. Before supper the monks washed again, then just before bedtime came the service of Compline. But at midnight, the bell which was seldom silent for long, tolled out again, and the monks, yawning and shivering, stumbled down the night stairs into the choir to sing the first office, that of Matins and Lauds. How thankfully they must have crawled on to their pallets once more for a few hours sleep before the bell woke them at sunrise once more for Prime.

Not that St Benedict had ever wished to prescribe anything burdensome, or even to regulate how much others should eat or drink, for he well understood that in the harsher climate of the West the extreme asceti-cism practised by Egyptian hermits could not be undertaken. 'Let a Cyrenean endure it if he will', one

Gallic monk protested. 'Necessity and Nature have accustomed him to eat nothing, but we Gauls cannot live in the manner of angels.' It was this moderation which no doubt appealed to the later Benedict of Aniane, when, during the reign of Charlemagne, the powers of Church and State united to attempt to impose uniformity as well as discipline upon the churches and monasteries of the empire. All monasteries were ordered to adopt the Rule of St Benedict of Nursia, as reformed by Benedict of Aniane. Although not entirely successful, these reforms did much for the spiritual unification of Christendom. After Charlemagne's death his empire disintegrated. Europe was again subjected to even more destructive raids from Scandinavians in the north, Saracens in the western Mediterranean, and from the eastern steppes the terrible Magyars overran Central Europe and North Italy.

But it was not only barbarians who destroyed churches and monasteries. The rapacity of feudal barons did equal harm by seizing the lands and goods of the church. A picture of Europe left by the prelates of Rheims in 909 could scarcely be painted in darker colours:

The cities are unpeopled, monasteries are in ruins or burned, the land is a desert. As the first men lived lawless lives, so today each man is a law to himself, despising the ordinances of God and man and of the Church. The great oppress the weak, the poor are violated, and the Church robbed of its possessions. Men, like the fish of the sea, devour each other. As to the monasteries, some have been destroyed by the heathen, others have been stripped of all they possess. The monks that remain follow no rule; they have no true abbots, owing to having submitted to secular

Odo, when the oratory of the monastery had been built, the brethren were unable to provide enough food for the large body of ministers who came with the bishop to consecrate the new building. However, a huge boar from the forest 'willingly offered itself to be slaughtered'. In this way their needs were miraculously provided for.

59 Monks showing their charter to a reforming abbot

Odo not only laid the foundations of Cluny's future greatness but was called upon by rulers and the Pope to reform other monasteries in France, Italy and in Rome itself. This was not an easy task, for monks disliked interference by abbots from other abbeys. At Fleury in France the monks forcibly resisted Odo's entry. An eye-witness described the scene. As Odo, attended by two bishops, approached the monastery, the monks, forewarned of his coming, barricaded the entrance. Then, arming themselves with swords and shields they went on to the roof of the building 'as though to hurl stones and missiles at their enemy'. Others, guarding the door, said they would rather die than admit the abbot from another monastery. Later they sent a deputation to show Odo their charters of independence. For three days the resistance continued, they even threatened to kill Odo. At last, unknown to anyone, the abbot mounted a donkey. On this humble steed, unattended and unarmed, he approached Fleury. Straightway the recalcitrant monks 'throwing away their arms went out to meet him and embraced his feet'. In such a fashion were these symbol-conscious monks of the Middle Ages won over to obedience by Odo's humility.

On another occasion the signs, hissings and facial contortions—which were used in lieu of speech when it was necessary to break the rule of silence—became a stumbling block to Odo and his reforming monks. One of Odo's party, a monk called Adolfus, was washing his shoes, preparatory to the rite of the washing of feet that was about to take place according to St Benedict's Rule. One of the 'unreformed' brethren passed by and saw him. 'Tell me where St Benedict orders monks to wash their shoes?' he asked Adolfus angrily. The brother made a sign for him to be quiet, as the monk was breaking the rule of silence. At that the monk even more angrily said, 'Who are you that come to preach the Rule to your betters? You pounce like a hawk on our property, and refuse to talk. God did not make me a serpent to hiss as you do, nor an ox that I should bellow. No. He made me a man with a tongue in my head—to talk with.' While he kept on barking out

remarks like this, St Odo's biographer tells us, Adolfus hurriedly retired.

St Odo was not blind to the evils of his time outside the monasteries. He fought the inhumanity, greed and ambition of the feudal magnates with the only weapon he possessed— fearless denunciation and spiritual example:

60   Abbot Hugh and Matilda of Tuscany intercede for Henry IV

Woe to you that are wealthy in Zion: you great men, heads of the people, that go in state with the house of Israel. . . . We should give honour, not to the rich for their fine clothes, but to the poor, the makers of such things, for the banquets of the powerful are cooked in the sweat of the poor.

His compassion for the poor and his faith in the power of forgiveness never failed Odo, even when he had suffered bodily injury at their hands. About the year 936 when Hugh, King of the Lombards, was besieging Alberic, ruler of Rome, Odo tried to make peace between them. As he went out on one of these missions, a yokel aimed a blow at his head. The bystanders, with a loud cry, seized the man by his hands. 'Then our most gentle father borrowed certain pennies and rendering good for evil sent his attacker away an ally.' When this affair came to the ears of the ruthless Alberic he wanted to cut off the yokel's hands. But Odo begged strenuously that this should not be done, and the man was saved from maltreatment.

Odilo, who ruled at Cluny from 994 to 1049, was a great builder. He claimed that he 'found an abbey of wood and left an abbey of marble'. Not only did he adorn the cloisters with columns of marble brought from the farthermost parts of the province but he also built a splendid gateway. Under Odilo, too, the Truce of God was proclaimed in 1042 in all the dioceses of France. He also wrote to the bishops of Italy, asking them to persuade the feudal magnates in their dioceses to accept it:

From the hour of vespers on Wednesday [this peace-making measure stated] until sunrise on Monday let there reign a settled peace and an enduring truce between all Christians, friends and enemies, neighbours and strangers so that for these four days and five nights, at all hours there may be safety for all men, so that they can devote themselves to business without fear of attack. . . .

Odilo's successor, Hugh, was above all a great statesman. He attended the courts of the King of France, of the emperor and of the Pope whenever important business was transacted. In the quarrel between the Emperor Henry IV and Pope Gregory VII, after Henry had been excommunicated, the emperor begged Hugh to intercede with the Pope for him. Small wonder then that Cluny's prestige and wealth increased. As a fitting symbol of this Hugh began the building of a great new basilica in 1088. The liturgy was also restored to its central place in the monastic life. Music, drama and art, all contributed to the beautifying of buildings and services. Indeed the offices of the Church and the celebration of the Mass were elaborated and dramatised, and such services as are found in the *Revelation of the Monk of Evesham* (really Eynsham) laid the foundation for the mystery and miracle plays, from which secular drama later developed. In the Office of the Sepulchre, for instance, the great cross of the Church was taken down and hidden behind the altar all Good Friday and Saturday. Then, before Matins on Easter Day, three white-robed figures, representing the Marys, advanced up the nave. From the tomb the angels' challenge rang out, 'What seek ye, O servants of Christ?' 'We seek Him who was crucified, O Host of Heaven,' came the reply. 'He is not here. He is risen. Go bear the tidings that He is risen from the tomb.'

For the Easter services the church was decked with tapestries on the walls and carpets over the benches. Exquisite frontals adorned the altars on which gold crucifixes, surrounded by images of the saints, were placed, lit by many-branched candelabra. The whole

church blazed with light, which glowed on the rich
vestments, on the gold of paten and chalice, on the
gleaming marble and jewels, and on the many-coloured
hangings and carpets. Up to the time of Abbot Hugh,
the zeal of the monks may have equalled all this
splendour. But the balance in monastic living, so
wisely placed there by St Benedict, had been destroyed.
Work had been cut out, to make room for the extended
liturgies. The abbot-statesmen no longer followed the
daily devotions, slept in the monks' dormitory, ate with
them in the refectory, or ruled them with the close
affection and understanding discipline of a father. The
greater part of an abbot's time was now spent in
litigation, to protect the worldly interests of abbeys, and
in playing a great part in the courts of Europe.

Nevertheless Cluny still had considerable influence
on the everyday life of laymen. The splendid liturgies
helped—even if somewhat indirectly—to counter-
balance the brutal and warlike character of the age. For
the practice was growing up among individual laymen
and women of devoting a part of their day to spiritual
exercises. To help them in this, they used some of the
simple and beautiful additions that had been made to
extend the liturgy in the monasteries. These, collected
together, were later to develop into the Books of Hours
which were so widely used in the later Middle Ages for
private devotions. Queen Margaret of Scotland
(*d.* 1033) always began her day by reciting some of these
short services. King Malcolm her husband, illiterate
and typical of most contemporary rulers and magnates,
was—like Duke William of Aquitaine—one of those
who, if unable himself 'to despise the things of this
world', nevertheless admired those whom he 'believed
to be righteous in the eyes of God'. He was known to
kiss and revere the sacred books used by his wife and
had her favourite volume bound in gold and jewels.

61   Abbots presenting their
monasteries to the Virgin

This is not to say that magnates were not keenly critical of the monasteries. William the Conqueror, accustomed to sending donations to the Abbey of Verdun whose abbot had been his father's friend, stopped sending gifts there on hearing that its discipline had grown lax. Laymen regarded monasteries as salt essential to the preservation of the rest of society; by their intercession eternal salvation for the souls of their benefactors and their kin could be ensured. A lax monastery was failing in these duties. Yet it was not the laxness of Cluniac monasteries which, about the opening of the twelfth century, led to criticism against them. It was rather the excess of zeal with regard to services and the adornment of their churches which caused the rise of a puritan party aiming at the restoration of the original simplicity and purity of the Benedictine Rule. The mouthpiece for this new demand for monastic reform was Stephen Harding. He was an English monk who had joined the Abbey of Molesme in Burgundy. Here the abbot was actively attempting to return to the simple and rigorous life of the early Benedictines. Harding supported him, and when the Englishman became the second abbot of Cîteaux he drew up, about 1117, a

Rule which was known as the Charter of Love. This gave an efficient organisation to what became known as the Cistercian Order of monks.

It was to St Bernard of Clairvaux, however, that the new order owed its rapid expansion. By the middle of the twelfth century there were almost 350 Cistercian houses in Europe. Some idea of the puritanical spirit of Cîteaux under St Bernard can be gained from his criticism of the beauties of the Abbey of Cluny:

> What is the object of all this? . . . the church walls are resplendent, but the poor are absent, . . . the curious find entertainment there, no doubt, but the wretched find within them no comfort for their misery. What has all this imagery to do with monks? What with those who profess poverty and spirituality of mind? As for the immense height of the churches, their immoderate length, their superfluous breadth, their costly marbles and strange designs, while they hinder the devotion of the worshipper, they remind me of Jewish ritual. This is all done for the glory of God it is said. But as a monk I demand 'Tell me, O Professors of Poverty, what does gold in a holy place?' . . . In fact such an endless variety of forms appear everywhere, that more time is spent in admiring these oddities than in meditating on the love of God. Before God, if they blush not before its wrongfulness, why do they not recoil from the expense?

St Bernard did not fail to apply these strict standards to his own life. His bare cell was so low that he could not stand upright in it, and he underwent such austerities that his health was permanently injured. After his death the Cistercian Order declined, largely because it began to grow immensely rich. Cîteaux was on the trading route via Brenner into Italy and commerce damaged the spiritual side of monastic life. While its

rentals grew longer, its prayers and austerities grew
shorter; though it developed a fleet for trading by river
and sea, it neglected its services for the poor. A contemporary poem pictures for us the activities of the
Cistercians during the period of decline.

> *Livings and churches they buy*
> *And many ways to cheat they try.*
> *They buy and sell at profit*
> *Awaiting settling day.*
> *And well they sell their corn*
> *And I have heard they do not scorn*
> *To lend their money to the Jews.*

Another reforming order which was established in
1084 was that of St Bruno in Savoy. In the monastic
foundation at Chartreux, each monk had his own small
house where he worked, cooked, ate, prayed, studied
and slept alone. The houses were placed round a courtyard, and all the buildings were enclosed by a wall.
Except when they met in church for Mass, or in
refectory where they gathered on Sundays and feast
days, the monks lived a solitary life in which the
Benedictine Rule of silence was most strictly kept.

St Bruno, writing to a friend of his youth after 25
years of life as a Carthusian monk said:

I live the life of a hermit, far from the haunts of men
on the borders of Calabria, with my brethren in
religion, some of them learned men. . . . What words
can describe the delights of this place—the mildness
and wholesomeness of the air . . . the hills rising
gently round, the shady valleys with their grateful
abundance of rivers, streams and fountains, the
well-watered gardens and useful growth of trees?
Why should I linger over these things? The delights
of the thoughtful man are more profitable than these,

for they are of God. . . . For only those who have
experienced the solitude and silence of a hermitage
know what profit and holy joy it confers on those who
love to dwell there.

The Carthusian Order was never very popular. Its
discipline was too strict. Those who followed it held to
its rules with such tenacity that it could truthfully be
said: 'It was never reformed because never deformed.'
During the twelfth century the cathedral schools
supplanted the monasteries as leaders of intellectual
life. Abelard, himself a monk, lamented the growing
worldliness of the cloister:

> We, who ought to live by the labour of our own
> hands (which alone St Benedict saith, maketh us
> truly monks), do now follow after idleness, that
> enemy of the soul, and seek our livelihood from the
> labours of other men . . . so that entangling ourselves
> in worldly business and striving under the sway of
> earthly covetousness to be richer in the cloister than
> we have been in the world, we have subjected our-
> selves to earthly lords, rather than to God. . . . We
> take from great men of this world in the guise of
> alms, manors, tenants, bondsmen and bondswomen
> . . . and to defend these possessions we are bound to
> appear in outside courts before worldly judges.

The possession of property, indeed, not only engrossed
monks in secular business, but attracted to monasteries
those with no true sense of vocation, especially those
wanting protection and maintenance, and landless
younger sons of the upper classes whose fathers used
influence to gain abbacies for them. But criticism of
monastic laxity came not only from clerics like Abelard,
but also from the towns where developing trade had
produced a new society. As early as 1058 a reforming

movement started in Milan and other Italian cities. Here, weavers, traders and townsfolk rebelled against the worldliness of bishops and nobles. Fifty years later, in the Low Countries, the working people of the weaving trade criticised their leaders in both Church and State, and proclaimed that sacraments administered by simoniac priests—those who had bought and sold ecclesiastical preferments—or by married priests were invalid.

In many cases these criticisms led to the emergence of heretical movements in the Church. There was a demand that she should return to the poverty of primitive Christianity, and renounce all worldly wealth and power. When in 1143 the commune of Rome rose against the Pope, Arnold of Brescia, one of the leading figures of reform in Italy, threw in his lot with the rebels. But, with the help of the Emperor Frederick II, the Papacy overthrew the revolution and Arnold was executed as a heretic.

The Poor Men of Lyons or Waldenses, headed by Peter Waldo, emerged about 1175. This sect denounced the holding of property and went about preaching the Gospel and translating the New Testament into the language of the people; as a result many were converted to a belief in their ideas.

The Albigensians, on the other hand, discarded the Christian faith, declaring that the Jehovah whom the Catholics worshipped was a power of evil. Both Waldensians and Albigensians were strong in the south of France, especially around Toulouse. When the Count of Toulouse took up their cause, the Papacy realised its danger. Pope Innocent III in 1208 preached a Crusade against the heretics. He declared that the lands of the count would be given to those orthodox princes who helped to conquer them. As a result, Languedoc, an exceptionally gay, cultured and prosperous part of

France, was subjected to one of the cruellest and most bloodthirsty campaigns in history. By the end of the century the frowning fortress-cathedral of Albi and the new university of Toulouse kept guard over a land rendered desolate and de-populated.

It was obvious that, with the emergence of a critical, mentally-alert population in the towns, a fresh approach to the people was needed on the part of the Church, especially as the parish clergy were often almost illiterate. Langland in the fourteenth century portrays Sloth as a parson devoted only to the gathering of tithes and to hunting, scarcely able to read his Mass-book. In the next century Erasmus' Fishmonger complains: 'Among the whole batch of priests there are scarce two or three tolerable persons, and many are scarce fit for the plough-tail.' Certainly priests of the calibre of Chaucer's Poor Parson were rare, both morally and numerically, especially in the towns, as the parochial organisation had been established when society was mainly rural. Most monasteries, also, had been built in the country and monks—officially at least—were bound to remain within the cloister. With the coming of the friars, however, these deficiencies

62 Friars

were met. They regarded the world as their parish. Unencumbered by possessions, without permanent homes, their declared aim was to preach Christ's gospel of Love, Peace and Holy Poverty.

St Francis of Assisi (55) founder of the order which later took his name, was one of the most lovable and attractive figures of the Middle Ages. In many ways his aims were the same as those of the Poor Men of Lyons. Partly for this reason, when Francis asked the Pope's permission in 1223 to follow his apostolic form of life Honorius III hesitated but finally gave way. Yet, before his death in 1226, St Francis realised the dangers facing his followers, many of whom wished to abandon their life of poverty and to use the wealth, now pouring in, to build churches and friaries. St Francis' appeal to them clearly testifies to his unshaken convictions:

I, little Brother Francis, desire to follow the life of poverty of Jesus Christ, persevering to the end. And I beg and exhort you, always to follow His most holy life of poverty. Take care never to depart from it upon the teaching of anyone whatsoever.

Shortly after his death, a stately church began to arise at Assisi. Today, two splendid basilicas, one above another, shelter the remains of the 'Little Brother' who, in life, so often had used a mere hovel for his home.

St Dominic (55), who had begun as a preacher among the Albigensians of Languedoc, was the founder of another order of friars. Joined by others—eager as himself to fight heresy—St Dominic gained the Pope's approval for his work in 1214; by 1221 the order had 60 monasteries scattered over western Europe. Realising that intellectual training and wide reading was necessary when refuting heretical opinions, St Dominic's followers were well educated. They later became a great teaching order. It was to them also that the

63   Plato and Socrates

powers of the Inquisition gradually passed. By 1258
two Dominicans held commissions as papal inquisitors
at Albi in southern France, while others were working
in Italy and Aragon in a similar capacity.

But, if the Dominicans became great persecutors of
heretics, the Franciscans within a century of their
leader's death had become the objects of persecution.
Whereas most Franciscans rapidly succumbed to the
temptation St Francis had warned them against—the
acquisition of wealth and property for their order—a
small number, the 'Spirituals', remained true to their
vows. These quickly became an object of derision. St
Bonaventura complains in 1266: 'St Francis cries
aloud to us to reform. For those brethren who remain
true to their vows, far from being looked up to as
examples, are now treated as laughing stocks.' By the
fourteenth century they were being persecuted as

heretics, and subjected to nameless tortures in convent
dungeons. Finally, in 1317, Pope John XXII declared
it heresy for a friar to disobey his immediate superior.
In 1318 four Spirituals were burned as heretics at
Marseilles for declaring that the Rule of St Francis was
identical with Christ's Gospel. These spiritual friars
begged permission to found a separate congregation of
their own. This was refused. The day was past when
the papacy was active in support of reform, or at least,
not hostile to it, consequently the evangelical spirit in
the friars' movement was sacrificed to the necessities
of power politics. Reform, henceforth, was to be mainly
anti-papal. This—a tragedy for Europe—helps to
account for the stagnation, spiritual and intellectual,
which so soon followed the twelfth-century renaissance.

At the same time the deterioration in the ranks of the
friars themselves also contributed. By the fourteenth
century Chaucer's and Langland's portraits of disreputable friars appear to have been justified: Langland's Dr Friar Flatter, alias Father Creep-into-Houses,
was admitted into the bedroom of Contrition, who was
ill:

> The friar gave him a fresh dressing, called Private
> Subscription. 'And I shall pray for you and your
> loved ones all my life.' To another patient he said
> 'I shall remember you in my Masses and Matins . . .
> for a small fee, of course.'

Begging and selling absolutions became so closely
associated with friars that many fled from them on
sight. Nevertheless, there were other humble friars like
St Bernadino who followed the ascetic ideals of St
Francis. The saint's worn face, with humour latent in
eyes and mouth, witnesses to the life he followed. Like
his master, he preached compassion and love. His
eloquence and warm humanity drew thousands to his

preaching. 'Perfection is this', he taught: 'On seeing a leper, you feel such compassion for him that you would rather bear his sufferings yourself, than that he should.'

St Bernadino was three times tried for heresy. On the last occasion Pope Eugenius IV indignantly swept the charge away, declaring the friar to be 'the most illustrious preacher and unerring teacher of all who are preaching the Gospel, in Italy or abroad'.

When, in 1444, Bernadino died, Europe had reached a turning-point in its history. During the next hundred years the medieval period was gradually emerging into that which we have termed 'modern'. Perhaps the most important single motive force which made possible this development was the preservation, the reconquest and the dissemination of Greek thought, especially that of Aristotle. The early monks had done most for the preservation of ancient manuscripts. But it was mainly in the cathedral schools and the universities into which they developed that the ancient learning was chiefly assimilated and then enlarged upon. On those medieval foundations the intellectual achievements, the work of scientists, the voyages of explorers and the art of the modern age were built.

7

SCHOOLS AND SCHOLARS

> There descended upon Neustria (Northern France) a pagan race from across the seas who, arriving in huge, beaked boats bared the sword of iniquity and wickedly laid waste almost the whole country. They destroyed many monasteries and churches with devouring flames; towns which were captured were razed to the ground, and Christians, they either killed or enslaved, selling them into everlasting bondage.

THIS description by a French monk of a single raid by Norse pirates gives some idea of the conditions with which Europeans of the eighth to tenth centuries had to contend. Yet, in spite of attacks like this, monasteries and cathedrals, with their schools and libraries, managed not only to survive, but to save and protect many ancient manuscripts and treasures. They were, indeed, storm-swept islands of culture, withstanding through the strength of faith, complete submersion beneath the wild floods of barbarism which surrounded them.

If given timely warning of a raid, the monks snatched up their precious books and holy vessels to carry them into the forests, or to some other safer retreat, until danger was past. When in 925, the wild Magyars swept over the Alpine passes and descended on the monastery of St Gall, near Lake Constance in modern Switzerland, all its inhabitants fled to the neighbouring and rival house of Reichenau—except for Heribald. He, somewhat weak in the head, refused to leave, because the chamberlain had not given him his allowance of shoe-leather for the year! The Magyars, uglier than the Danes but better natured, began to break up the winecasks. 'Stop! Stop!' shouted Heribald. 'What are we to drink when you have gone away?' They roared with laughter, but surprisingly desisted. Yet, when the simple monk reproved them for talking in church, they beat him up. Later they repented and, plied him with wine, which more than made up for the beating. 'I never remember cheerier souls', Heribald said later. 'But wild! So wild in cloister and church, they might have been beasts in the forest.'

As soon as the Magyars left, the monks returned with their manuscripts. Among them was a copy of Priscian's grammar book, originally written in the first half of the sixth century A.D. Judging by its delicate Irish script it had been made by the monks of Clonfert or Clonmacnoise. They had been forced to flee from the attacks of Norsemen and the Priscian had been taken first to Cologne—for during those troubled times books and their rescuers travelled far. By the tenth century it had reached St Gall where it once more escaped destruction, returning again to rest in peace in the monastery for the next 900 years. Indeed it can still be seen there among other treasured possessions. It was mainly through the efforts of devoted Benedictine monks that our rich heritage of classical learning and literature was preserved in the West.

Only towards the end of the tenth century when the raids of the Norsemen were ceasing could Europe attempt any serious rebuilding of her culture and education. This was founded on one of the most fundamental beliefs of the Middle Ages—the belief that society was, by divine dispensation, divided into three classes: those who fought and governed, those who prayed (57), and those who toiled with their hands (56). An early thirteenth-century poem expresses this idea:

> *The work of a clerk is earnest prayers,*
> *And justice must flow from chevaliers,*
> *While labourers toil for their bread.*
> *In church, in town, in field—all three*
> *By ordination all agree.*

Education was therefore designed to fit the child for his appropriate station in life, were he nobleman, cleric or artisan.

The children of aristocrats sometimes learned their letters at their mother's knee. St Louis of France was one of these, being taught to read by Queen Blanche of Castile from her psalter (which is still in existence), while in 1454 Charles Duke of Berry, aged eight, owned five school books—an ABC, a copy of the Seven Penitential Psalms, Donatus' *Minor Grammar*, Cato's *Moral Sayings* and a rhymed version of Priscian's *Grammar*. Sometimes the lord's household chaplain taught the children rudiments of Latin and how to read and write. But in the Middle Ages good manners were considered more essential than an ability to read. A thirteenth-century poem taught that:

> *A good child upright he must stand,*
> *Before his lord when he doth eat,*
> *Nor scratch his limbs with either hand,*
> *And if a great gift or a small is given,*
> *While kneeling he must render thanks.*

It was also necessary to become proficient at chess and backgammon, to hawk, hunt and fence, to study geometry, magic and law. A French romance *Aiol* describes the ideal education for a young aristocrat:

> His father made him ride through wood and meadow, to learn how to trot and ride a horse. . . . Aiol knew about the courses of the stars and the changes of the moon. Moses the hermit schooled him in letters, writing and speaking both Latin and French.

Very often boys and girls of the upper classes were sent to other households to be trained. From about seven years of age boys served as pages, then from 14 as squires. The girls acted as companions to the lady of the household and were taught the arts of spinning, weaving and embroidery, as well as those of household management.

At the other end of the scale, peasants and artisans, unless they had outstanding ability and entered a monastic school, did not receive any formal education beyond that necessary for taking part in services at church. Their function was to provide bread and food for themselves and their masters and to keep the wheel of day-to-day existence rotating.

Up to about A.D. 1100, education in northern Europe was largely in the hands of the monks. Schools existed mainly for oblates—boys destined to become monks. But some monasteries ran an external school where boys not so dedicated were taught. Children were often handed over as oblates very young and never saw their parents again. Orderic Vitalis, a twelfth-century chronicler, was one of these. He tells us that he was baptised one Easter Eve:

> When 5 years old I became a scholar at Shrewsbury and dedicated my first lessons to you, O God, in the church of St Peter and St Paul. The well-known

priest, Sigward, taught me my letters, psalms, hymns and other learning. . . . Then, fearing that affection for my parents might deflect me from your worship, you led my father Odeler to give me entirely to you. Weeping, he gave me, a weeping child to Rainald the monk, sent me into exile for your love and never saw me again. A small boy did not presume to withstand his father, so I left my country, my parents, my kindred and friends who wept bitterly at the parting.

I was 10 when I crossed the Channel to Normandy —an exile—unknown and friendless. Yet by your grace, O God, strangers gave me kindness and friendship. I was received into the monastery of St Evroul at Ouche, near Lisieux and tonsured in clerkly manner. I was renamed Vitalis and have lived 56 years in this abbey. . . .

Not all children settled so happily into the monastic life to which their parents dedicated them. In the ninth century Gottschalk, a knight's young son, was brought to the monastery of Fulda to be trained as a monk. His restless spirit refused to be tamed; constantly he rebelled and was as constantly punished. At 16 he begged for freedom. A council of bishops acquiesced, but his abbot, stern and adamant, appealed to the emperor. Gottschalk was condemned by him for life to the Order of St Benedict.

Yet another oblate, a French peasant's son—Gerbert —by the brilliance of his teaching brought fame to the monastic school of Reims. Scholars came from all over Europe to sit at his feet. By revolutionising the medieval system of education Gerbert, who in 999 became Pope Sylvester II, paved the way for the splendours of the twelfth-century 'renaissance' in Europe.

Up to 972 when, having absorbed the scientific

learning of Italy and the Spanish march, Gerbert moved to Reims, teaching in schools had been dull and repetitive. Books were scarce, usually only the master was supplied with one. The curriculum, following that of Roman times, consisted of the Seven Liberal Arts, divided into the *Trivium* and *Quadrivium*. The first division consisted of grammar, rhetoric and logic. These subjects had to be mastered before proceeding to the

64 Rhetoric teaches the art of speaking by a tree of rules

study of arithmetic, geometry, astronomy and music, which comprised the *Quadrivium*. Grammar was taught from text-books by Donatus (a fourth-century writer) and Priscian (sixth-century). The subject included learning by heart Cato's *Moral Sayings*, passages of Virgil and Ovid, with those from other writers, both pagan and sacred. Pupils also learned to write with styluses on wax tablets and, when they became more proficient, with quills on parchment. Latin was compulsory for all conversation during school hours. Punishments for breaking rules were severe, yet we know that masters had their less strict moments when discipline, even in monasteries, was relaxed. This is illustrated by an episode in the novices' school at St Gall, where Salomon was a famous abbot in the tenth century. Although a strict disciplinarian, he was a man of great charm and understanding. On the Feast

Day of the Holy Innocents, when scholars were habitually allowed great freedom, the boys captured the lord abbot himself. Carrying him off to the school-room they put him into the master's chair.

With a mischievous twinkle Salomon said, 'You have made me your master. Very well! I will exact a penalty. Strip, all of you', and he picked up the master's birch. Crestfallen, the boys exchanged glances, then one of the brightest cried, 'Sir! It is the custom that, if we can make up, on the spur of the moment, a verse which pleases you, we can claim exemption from our beating.' The abbot nodded. At once, two boys composed rhyming couplets so apt, that Salomon, embracing them, gave the whole school three days' holiday with feasting at the abbey's expense, and that not for one year only, but for all time.

But at Reims, Gerbert, without sacrificing discipline, introduced both originality and depth into the teaching of the subjects of the *Quadrivium*. Arithmetic, which up to then had been most sketchily taught, he revolutionised by his introduction of the nine Hindu-Arabic numerals—1, 2, 3, 4, 5, 6, 7, 8, 9—hitherto never used outside Moslem Spain and Sicily in western Europe. Small wonder that schoolboys had quailed when faced with an addition in Roman numerals such as £MCMLXXX XV*s*. X*d*. and £MMCCCLX X*s* I*d*. By reviving the use of the abacus, a rectangle divided into columns for digits, tens and hundreds, and making the counters with the new numbers, the solving of arithmetical problems became much simpler. When representing the number 304, for instance, in the abacus columns, a counter numbered 3 was placed in the hundred column, the tens column was left empty and a 4 counter was put into the digit column. As, however, the use of the zero sign '0' was not introduced into western Christendom until later, the writing down of a number such as 304 caused complications. In fact it was often mistakenly entered in accounts as 34. The Hindus used a symbol for zero, but it is not known how long it was before one was used in the West. The work which, when translated into Latin, first brought a knowledge of the Arabic mathematical system to western Christendom had been written by a certain Al Khowarizmi. The study which we now

65   Between a mathematician and a computist sits an astronomer. In one hand he holds an astrolabe (for calculating the elevation of the stars), in the other an early telescope

call arithmetic was first known as *algorism*, from his name. Yet, in spite of its manifest superiority over the cumbersome system of Roman numeration, algorism and Arabic-Hindu numerals took four centuries from their first introduction to establish themselves in the West. Leonard of Pisa's *Book of the Abacus*, produced in 1202, advocated the system, but it was John Holywood's *Algorismus*, employing Arabic numerals, which later in the century helped to popularise their use.

In addition to promoting an improvement in the teaching of arithmetic, Gerbert believed that the theory of each subject should be demonstrated whenever possible in a practical manner. For lessons in music he advocated the use of the *organistrum*—a sort of hurdy-gurdy—and recommended a monochord to gain correct pitch. Astronomy he enlivened by demonstrating with spheres, on which the position and

movement of the stars could be shown. For observing
the heavens he also invented a tube which was a
primitive forerunner of the telescope. Gerbert's own
fame was such that it was said that he could calculate
the distance between points on earth and in the sky
'just by looking'.

Perhaps his most important contribution to education was to enlarge the study of logic and rhetoric, or
the art of public speaking, which had held such pro-
minence in imperial days. Gerbert declared:

> I have always studied both to live well and to speak
> well. For although the former is more important
> than the latter . . . yet in public affairs, both are
> necessary. To be able to persuade and restrain with
> words the wills of lawless men is useful in the highest
> degree.

Gerbert encouraged the use of Aristotle's books on
logic, which had been translated into Latin by the sixth-
century philosopher, Boethius, whose book *On the
Consolations of Philosophy* was popular throughout the
Middle Ages. So greatly did the young emperor
Otto III admire this scholar, that he hung Boethius'
portrait in his palace. Otto, half-Saxon, half-Greek,
was also greatly influenced by Gerbert. In October 997
he wrote to that 'most skilled of masters, crowned in the
three branches of philosophy' (physics, ethics and
logic), asking him to become his tutor:

> We desire you to show your aversion to Saxon
> ignorance by stimulating our Greek subtlety to zeal
> for study. . . . We humbly ask that the flame of your
> knowledge may sufficiently fan our spirit, until with
> God's aid, you cause the lively genius of the Greeks to
> shine forth.

Gerbert granted Otto's request and together the delicate, imaginative boy and the scholarly cleric-politician set out not only to emulate Charlemagne and Alcuin by a revival of ancient learning, but also to restore if possible the glories of the Roman Empire.

66   The philosopher Boethius

By the eleventh century, education had passed largely into the hands of the secular clergy in the schools which were developing in the cathedrals under the control of their bishops. Those at Chartres, Tours, Paris, Rouen, Liège and Utrecht were among the most famous. On the façades of some of these cathedrals stand sculptured figures symbolising the Seven Liberal Arts. At Notre Dame in Paris, Grammar is seen as an old woman with a rod, Dialectic with the serpent of Wisdom, Rhetoric carries the tablets of poetry. The *Quadrivium* is represented by Arithmetic counting on her fingers, Geometry holding compasses, Astronomy with an astrolabe, while Music is striking a peal of bells with a hammer.

At Chartres, Bishop Fulbert, a pupil of Gerbert's, helped to establish his great master's educational system. Fulbert, always interested in the study of medicine, put the principles of Hippocrates into verse to help students memorise them. The *Capitularies* of Charlemagne and some Canon and Roman law were

also taught and scholars came from far and wide to his
school.

About 1140 John of Salisbury—later to become one
of the shining lights of the twelfth-century renaissance
—studied there. He deplored the growing neglect of
grammar in the schools. One of the greatest teachers,
John tells us, was Bernard of Chartres:

> the most illustrious scholar in Gaul in modern times.
> His method was to read and point out what was
> simple and tallied with the rules. His aim, to dispense
> learning according to his pupils' mental capacity.
> . . . Since memory is improved and talent sharpened
> by use, he encouraged some by reproofs, but others
> by blows and penalties.

This reference to corporal punishment (*67*) shows
that the school at Chartres was below university grade,
since no record of physical chastisement at universities
has been recorded before the fifteenth century. John
goes on to tell us that the *Declinatio*, the last exercise of
the day, was so stuffed with grammar that if anyone
took it for a full year, unless he were a complete dullard,
he would have acquired the principles of speaking and
writing and could not remain ignorant of the meaning
of words in common use.

But John notes with amusement mixed with fore-
boding that many students and masters regarded their
predecessors as old-fashioned:

> *On all sides they shout: Where is this old donkey going?*
> *Why does he speak of the sayings and deeds of the ancients?*
> *We have inside information; our youth is self-taught.*
> *Our set does not accept these out-moded dogmas.*
> *We can't be bothered to follow the precepts*
> *Of those authors whom Greece has and Rome reveres.*

I reside near the Petit Pont, a new author in arts,
I glory in making discoveries of my own.
What my forerunners taught but dear youth knows not yet—
I swear is the offspring of my own mind.
A worshipping crowd of students surrounds me.
Believing my astounding statements to be very truth.

In Italy, schools of rhetoric, modelled on those of imperial Rome, never perished; it was largely through them that European law and politics were preserved. Here the tradition of lay scholarship had persisted, here both masters and students were not always, as elsewhere in Europe, clerics. This was why, when later the early schools developed into universities, Italy took the lead in secular studies, so that Bologna and Salerno became the greatest centres of law and medicine, whereas Paris reigned as queen of theology.

This development occurred at the beginning of the twelfth century through the brilliance of several great teachers. In Bologna these were Irnerius and Gratian. Irnerius was described as 'the lamp of the law and the first to throw light on the science', while Gratian, about 1140, wrote his famous book the *Decretum*. This aimed at clarifying the confused collections of canon law, those rules relating to faith, morals and discipline which had been drawn up through the centuries to regulate Church government. In Paris, it was chiefly William of Champeaux

67 Chastisement of a scholar

and Peter Abelard who, as teachers of philosophy, drew eager students in crowds to their schools. Later, France was to be described as 'the oven where the intellectual bread of the whole world was baked'.

68   Pillar capital of Abelard and Heloise

One of Abelard's letters reveals the jealousies that existed in these schools, and the rivalries of competing masters, before students and doctors had formed themselves into a guild (*universitas*), out of which the universities directly developed. Abelard tells us that his father

had been educated in letters before he began his military training. Indeed, he was so devoted to literature that he wished his sons to be instructed in letters before they were trained in arms. Because I was his firstborn and most dear, he took particular pains with my education. For my part, the more I learned, the more I became devoted to study. I journeyed through various provinces, disputing wherever the art of logic was flourishing.

Finally I reached Paris where this subject was taught by William of Champeaux, then prominent in this field, actually and by reputation. Studying under him I was first welcomed but later heartily disliked when I tried to refute some of his statements and sometimes proved his superior in argument. Those regarded as leading scholars were indignant (at my temerity) since I was regarded as junior both in years and time of study.

At last, presuming upon my ability . . . I a mere youth, desired to have my own classes and chose the celebrated town and royal seat of Melun where I should do so. William, hearing of this first tried to separate my pupils from his, before I had left Paris. He also tried to prevent my teaching in Melun. But William's enemies, among the powers that be, supported me, and his obvious jealousy won others to my side, so that I was able to carry out my purpose.

By the end of the twelfth century many cathedral schools had developed into universities, including those at Salerno, Bologna, Paris, Montpellier and Oxford. The word *universitas* meant a guild. The northern universities followed the example of Paris, where it was the masters who banded themselves into guilds to safeguard their rights. In the southern universities of Europe, on the other hand, it was the students who took this initiative.

In 1215, by a special mandate from the Pope, rules were drawn up to regulate conditions and to try to avert the friction to which Abelard refers. One of these laid down that: 'No one shall lecture in the arts at Paris before he is 21 years of age and he shall have

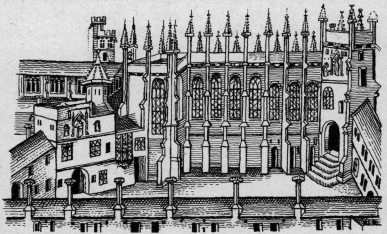

69   New College, Oxford, in the fourteenth century

heard lectures for at least six years before he begins to lecture.'

For theology the terms were even stricter. A lecturer had to be 35 before lecturing and to have studied for eight years at least. The right to teach at all was carefully guarded.

In Italy, the chief officer of the guild of students was the rector. He corresponded to a chief magistrate in an Italian town. Appointed by the votes of students, not of the doctors and masters of the university, he had technically to be a cleric. His prestige can be judged by the fact that at public functions he took precedence over even a cardinal.

After the installation of the rector, a great banquet was held. Then, an account of 1444 tells us:

> students turned to games and gala making . . . dances or jousting. At Ferrara, after the assumption of his cap by the new rector, the students in arts in the house of Niccolo Passetti which was located in the street of Santa Maria Novella held a noble banquet and public dances. They then set up in the street the wooden image of a man, called in the vernacular Bamboccio or 'Little Doll' and tilted against it with spears. A prize was given to the victor, who was applauded by all the banqueteers and spectators.

A rector was no autocratic governor, but ruled by the advice of a council and was bound to observe the statutes of the university; students could always claim redress against illegal actions on the part of their rector. In 1433 a student of civil law at Florence complained that Hieronymus the rector had bought six measures of grain from him at the customary price. Not until four months later did Andreas receive any payment and then only seven pounds. When asked for the balance he was given a book of medicine, 'for which', he said, 'I received five florins'.

Some time later the rector asked for the return of the book. 'Pay what you owe me and I will gladly give you the book', Andreas said. But the rector, 'puffed up with pride,' answered, 'You will return the book to me without my paying you.' To add insult to injury, Hieronymus later sent the servant of a magistrate to seize Andreas, who was attending a lecture. There, before his fellow-students, Andreas was seized 'with vituperation thus branding him with disgrace, and was flung into the town prison like any common thief'. Andreas demanded that a severe fine should be levied on the rector, 'not only because of his personal wrongs, but because the scholar's dress he wore had been insulted and through him the University itself'. His demand was granted. The rector was ordered to pay to Andreas £20 as well as costs.

This matter of academic dress was important. Regulations were drawn up by the universities to enforce 'decency of garb'. Both 'masters who do not shrink from attending disputations in their mantles, sleeveless tunics or tabards' and bachelors or scholars who presumed to take their seats in other costumes than the long-sleeved cope (*cappa*) were frowned upon. It was decreed, therefore, that 'masters should come to disputations in proper dress, namely, in cope, cassock long or short, trimmed with fur'. Students had to wear closed over-tunics with long sleeves and an upper tunic. At the university of Paris in the fourteenth century the four faculties of arts, medicine, jurists and theologians were assigned distinct costumes for their representatives:

Artists go forth in black and round copes of noble brunet [a cloth made of dyed wool] or of fine perse, or blue cloth lined with fur. Medical students wore copes the colour of thick rouge. Jurists wore scarlet. The reverend master of theology, if regular clergy, were clad in the copes of their Order; if they were seculars, in any simple garb of humble colour.

In the early days of universities there were no hostels for students. John of Salisbury, writing with gratitude to a friend, reminded him of his own youthful difficulties as a poor student in Paris:

It is not the first time you have procured supplies of food for me. Your kindness of old when you found me poor made me feel that I lacked neither a father's nor a mother's love. It was a great achievement to make such provision for an exile so that I enjoyed the benefits of a citizen in a foreign land.

During the twelfth century, however, colleges were founded for poor scholars. The earliest of these was the College of the Eighteen founded in Paris by an Englishman in 1180. Here the students' lodging was a room in the Hospice of the Blessed Mary for the poor and sick. A bed was provided for each, together with a small allowance of money. In return the scholars had to take it in turn to carry the cross and holy water before the bodies of those who died in the Hospice. 'Each night also', the rule continued, 'the clerks must celebrate

70   Students of St Mary's Hospice

seven penitential psalms with due prayers instituted as
of old.'

Such students were not always grateful for the benefits they received. In 1228 we are told:

> certain poor scholars of St Thomas of the Louvre,
> who for long past had lived on the goods of that house,
> had reached such a point of insolence that, unless
> they were received at night, they broke in violently,
> and entered the house of the brothers. Others ate
> more than was expedient for those studying a long
> time, making little progress and disturbing the quiet
> and study of others.

It was finally found necessary to help only those
whose conduct was meritorious. The contentious, the
quarrelsome and evil-livers were deprived of their
benefits, since:

> we have no intention of providing for the perverse,
> lazy, ribald gamesters, and haunters of taverns, but
> only for the good and true scholars through whom
> provision may be made for the church and the
> salvation of souls.

These scholars had also to submit to a weekly
examination to discover if their work was up to
standard. They received lodging and an allowance of
money in some cases for one year only. This was
renewed at the discretion of the foundationers. But they
received many extra privileges, such as being allowed
to borrow standard manuscripts for the purpose of
copying them without payment—other than repeating
seven psalms for the soul of the defunct donor of the
MS. and a tip to its custodian of one penny; whereas a
wealthier student had to give a pledge of gold before
the manuscript was lent to him, as well as pay a rent
for the use of the manuscript according to the number

of pages it contained. Regulations which tried to cover
every contingency were made for university students.
They had to attend lectures in a closed overtunic, with
an upper tunic.

But open over-tunics, togas and hoods may be worn
by students when not attending academic functions
or when eating outside their own lodgings. Sleeveless
vests—woollen close-fitting under-garments—may
not be worn, nor may ornate mittens, shoes and
berets. If anyone wishes to go on horseback or for
exercise, he may wear what he pleases. . . .

Lectures began early. A student had to rise on hearing the bells for early Mass. This was usually about
sunrise but the time varied according to the season of
the year. He then had to hasten to attend ordinary
lectures for two hours. At first these were given in a
hired hall, sometimes in a church, or in the doctor's
own home. Later, special lecture rooms were built. A
regulation issued in 1358 by the dauphin of France to
the university of Paris throws a lurid light on conditions
there.

We make known to men [Charles begins] that,
although to our beloved sons, the masters and
scholars studying at Paris in the faculty of arts from
the first foundation of the university, or almost so,
the Street of Straw was assigned to masters and
scholars for the purpose of giving and hearing
lectures, and in times past these were given in peace,
now with increasing malice of men and the enemy of
science [knowledge] sowing tares among the wheat,
in the said street at night filth and refuse are brought
and left there, which corrupt the hearts and bodies
of those dwelling there. What is more horrible . . . at

night the entrances to the schools are broken in by panders and foulest men who desire to impede the pearl of science. Impure women are also brought into the schools so that in the morning, when masters and scholars come there they find such a disgraceful and stinking mess that they flee from such a fetid, horrible and impure place.

The dauphin then agreed that gates should be erected at both ends of the Street of Straw; if these were locked at night the misuse of the lecture rooms could be prevented.

When a freshman—called a *bajan*—became a scholar at a university, he had to undergo an ordeal known as the 'jocund advent'. Conditions regarding this varied in different places and at different times, but always involved feasting at the bajan's expense and a good deal of horse-play. Directions for a ceremony of the bajans are given in a document of the College of Annency at Avignon. An abbot was elected to preside over the Court of the Bajans. On arriving there the luckless freshmen had to stand with uncovered heads and to receive a blow from a ferrule. Under penalty of two further blows, they were ordered to keep quiet. A bajan who had served for a year, and was due to be purged of his base name, next had to expound a passage which his fellow-bajans must dispute with him. If he was successful the two bajans most recently purged brought water to wash and purge the new candidate who, after his purging, was led through the town on an ass. The Bajans' Court met twice a week and could impose penalties on those who had warmed themselves at the fire in hall when seniors were present, or who had called his senior a bajan or had failed in his duties at table.

At German universities the bajan was treated as a wild

animal who had to be tamed. The ceremonies included
the removal of imaginary horns, tusks and claws by use
of augers, saws and pincers, so that injury to the victim
was not always avoided. Consequently rules were
drawn up to try to prevent this. In Paris it was forbidden
to exact anything from a bajan unless it were a free-will
offering on the freshman's behalf to the students with
whom he lived. Any insult, attack or threat against a
bajan was to be divulged to the provost of Paris who
would have the offender punished.

Violence was an almost inescapable condition of
medieval life including that of students at the university. They fought not only among themselves, quarrel-
ling over dogs, slashing off one another's fingers with
swords, and rushing, with their tonsured heads un-
protected, into conflicts that would have made a fully
armed knight hesitate, but they also broke into houses,
attacked citizens and abused women. This led to many
town and gown conflicts in which noblemen and their
servants were involved.

In 1404, the university of Paris was at the height of
its powers and was able to call down exemplary punishment on one of its high-born oppressors. In that year a
university procession was on its way to the church of
St Catherine, patroness of scholars, to intercede for the
peace of Church and Realm and for the health of the
king. A party of pages and others in the service of the
king's chamberlain, Charles of Savoisy, on their way
to the Seine to water their horses, encountered the
procession. Refusing to stand aside, they rode on among
the scholars. At once an affray broke out, stones were
thrown, wounds inflicted and boys trampled beneath
the horses. Not content with this, the retainers rushed
back to the chamberlain's town house and seized
weapons, bows and arrows.

Returning, they drove the procession into a neighbouring church where Mass was being celebrated. At once a crowd of indignant clerics, headed by the university rector, sought the king. When they threatened to leave Paris if justice were not done, they were promised redress. Eventually this was given and Charles of Savoisy was fined 1,000 livres. This sum his victims received while another similar sum was devoted to the endowment of five chaplaincies which—held by the masters—had to remain in the gift of the university. Charles was also forced to relinquish his post as chamberlain, to leave the court and to have his town house destroyed. The triumphant scholars themselves performed the latter task and also saw to it that the three servants of Charles, who had instigated the original affray, were forced to walk barefoot to church as penitents, clad only in their shirts and carrying tapers in their hands. They were flogged *en route*, thus acting as whipping boys for their master.

Yet, if we hear of many violent scenes connected with student life, there are others just as peaceful, not to say idyllic. Some of these are re-created for us through the manuals providing descriptive vocabularies in Latin for students. For this was the language compulsory for all conversations at the university. The manuals open windows which look out over these distant centuries. Through them we can follow the French student Jean as he hurries from quarter to quarter in Paris. We see him lingering by the bookstalls of Parvis Notre Dame; then, crossing to the market of Rue Neuve nearby, he purchases a broiled fowl for his supper. After crossing the Grand Pont he hurries past the goldsmiths' shops on either side and the tables of the money-changers. At the saddler's he stops again to look longingly at the saddles and elegant gloves displayed. The cobbler's shop reminds him to collect a pair of shoes he had left to be repaired. Then he calls at the apothecary's to buy some powder for a stomach upset, caused perhaps by the notoriously bad eggs of Paris.

The shop that sold candles, also sold writing materials. After making purchases there, Jean, driven by hunger and thirst, hastens to the Latin Quarter. Here, hawkers of wine, fruit-sellers and vendors of light pastry, with covered baskets of wafers, waffles and rissoles, are busy shouting their wares. But it is to the patisserie that Jean hurries. Here he can just afford to buy a plate of tripe and sausages. Not for him the tarts filled with eggs and cheese, highly spiced pork-pies, the chicken and eels which wealthier students are devouring at a table opposite. Then, after wiping his plate and knife clean with a crust of bread and eating it, he goes out in search of an alehouse to quench his thirst.

Through another of our linguistic windows we see Carl at Heidelberg. Here the setting is different. The scene—the banks of the Neckar, where the famous philosopher's road, which has charmed so many Heidelberg students, is being followed by Carl and his friend. As they walk they exchange remarks in Latin on birds, trees or fishes. Or maybe they begin a fierce argument about 'realism' and 'nominalism', or perhaps Carl seeks his friend's advice on a letter he has just received from home bidding him to return to marry a wealthy and well-born lady. He tells his friend that he is reluctant to obey: 'It is foolish to desert the cause of learning for a woman, for one may always get a wife, but science once lost can never be recovered.'

Perhaps Carl is dejected because he is due to expound, and be examined on, his thesis for

71   A goliard takes vows of love

his doctorate before the archdeacon and doctors of his college. He is afraid he may be refused his licentiate. His friend advises him to give a feast to his examiners. If he treats them well they will be more lenient and vote in his favour. Then, at last, he will be led in honour to a master's chair, be presented with an open book, have a biretta placed on his head, and finally receive a bene-diction and the kiss of peace. The ceremony will be followed by a triumphal procession through the narrow streets of Heidelberg and back to his lodging, where he and his friends will celebrate his success with a great feast.

One somewhat disreputable branch of the scholastic fraternity was that of the *goliards* or wandering scholars. It was said of them that 'they roam from city to city . . . in Paris seeking the liberal arts, in Orleans classics, at Salerno medicine, at Toledo magic—but nowhere manners or morals.'

Their chief habitat was northern France, the centre of the twelfth-century renaissance. Goliardic poetry is frankly pagan, exulting in life, love and beauty. It reflects the gayer, less reputable but more zestful side of the life possible to an unconforming cleric. At way-side taverns they drank and sang their convivial songs:

> *We in our wandering*
> *Blithesome and squandering*
> *Tara, tantara, teino,*
> *Eat to satiety,*
> *Drink with propriety,*
> *Laugh till our sides we split,*
> *Rags on our hides we fit,*
> *Jesting eternally,*
> *Quaffing infernally,*
> *Tara, tantara, teino.*

Defiant, impudent and gay, often suffering great
hardship yet without self-pity, they were the despair
and exasperation of the Church. Nothing could make
the *goliard,* a born wanderer and seeker after pleasure
into a useful member of society. What could be done
with clerics who boasted:

> *Down the broad way do I go*
> *Young and unregretting,*
> *Wrap me in my vices up,*
> *Virtue all forgetting.*
> *Greedier for all delight*
> *Than heaven to enter in*
> *Since the soul in me is dead,*
> *Better save the skin.*

At last by 1231, her patience exhausted, the Church
decreed that any cleric found wandering was to be
shaven, his tonsure, the treasured sign of his privileged
class, to be removed. Moreover, any ecclesiastic giving
him help or refuge was himself to be fined or suspended.
After this the *ordo vagorum,* the society of wandering
scholars, deteriorated rapidly. Soon the word *goliard*
became a term of derision, then of degradation and by
the end of the fourteenth century had sunk to synony-
mity with 'brothel-keeper'.

The *goliards,* however, must not be confused with
wandering scholars of the calibre of John of Salisbury,
of Gerbert or Nicholas Breakspeare, the only Englishman ever to attain the Papal Chair. They, indeed,
journeyed from one great school in Europe to another,
thirsting not for excitement and pleasure but for
knowledge. Thousands of lesser students, with an
equal enthusiasm for learning, were also on the dusty
highways, burnt so brown in summer that their own
fathers did not know them. It is to these myriad scholars
that we owe the preservation of ancient, and the

creation of new, scholarship—and to the *goliards* the
flame of poetic imagination kept alive, as one of the
gems of secular Latin poetry well shows:

> *When Diana lighteth*
> *Late her crystal lamp,*
> *Her pale glory kindleth*
> *At her brother's fire;*
> *Little straying west winds*
> *Wander over heaven,*
> *Moonlight falleth*
> *And recalleth*
> *With a sound of lute strings shaken,*
> *Hearts that have denied his reign*
> *To Love again.*
> *Hesperus the evening star,*
> *To all things that mortal are,*
> *Grants the dew of sleep.*

8

CHURCH BUILDERS AND ARTISTS

'IN the Middle Ages, men had no great thought which they did not write down in stone.' This statement of Victor Hugo's is largely true. For there was the strongest possible link between the work of poets and scholars, of philosophers and theologians and that of church builders and artists. Medieval cathedrals contain illustrations, not only of Biblical and religious truths, but also—through the medium of art—of poems and popular legends, episodes in the lives of saints, scientific and philosophical beliefs and historical facts, as well as scenes from everyday life and that of nature.

Since schools were attached to many cathedrals where the most brilliant scholars of their day were teaching and studying, it was natural that the Seven Arts, or subjects of the *trivium* and *quadrivium*, should also be symbolised in churches. These, therefore, became not only the 'poor man's Bible' but illustrated encyclopedias as well. Within their walls, children, the uneducated, and, in early times, newly converted pagans could not only receive verbal instruction in the faith, but could also have its truths, legends and learning clarified and made more vivid through statues, paintings, stained glass and other forms of art.

The major artistic works of the Middle Ages were executed under the direction of the Church and a sort of symbolic code was established from early times to which artists adhered when portraying certain subjects.

Since it was only monks who had the necessary mathematical knowledge and artistic training to build and decorate the churches during the Dark Ages, it was they who continued early traditions and established new ones. By the thirteenth century, laymen were taking over both as builders and artists. Gradually, against the wish and often against the opposition of the Church, innovations crept in. From the earliest Christian centuries, however, a nimbus behind the head of a figure denoted sanctity. The addition of a cross to the nimbus indicated that the figure portrayed represented either God the Father or God the Son. On the tympanum at Chartres, Christ is shown with a nimbus and cross, with the auriole—a ray which, signifying sanctity, surrounds the whole body; the feet are bare because only God, Christ and the angels were so represented. The right hand is held up with thumb and two forefingers raised—the gesture of blessing—while surrounding the Christ are the four emblems of the evangelists—a man for St Matthew, the winged lion for St Mark, the winged bull for St Luke and the eagle for St John.

That artists were not intended to choose their own subjects is proved by the decree of the Fathers, assembling for the second Council of Nicaea in 787, which stated: 'The composition of religious imagery is not left to the initiative of the artists, but is formed upon principles laid down by the Catholic Church and by religious tradition.' All through the medieval centuries it was intended that this decree should hold good. In 1425, when the chapter of the Church of the Madeleine at Troyes wanted a series of tapestries illustrating the history of their patron saint, the artists were given their subjects:

Brother Didier, the Dominican Friar, having extracted and given in writing the history of the holy Magdalen, Jaquet, the painter, made a small sketch of it on paper. Then the seamstress, Poinsette, with her assistant, collected great bed-sheets to serve for the executing of the models, which were painted by Jaquet the painter and Simon the illuminator.

Brother Didier, while taking wine with the artists, discussed the execution of the work with them. So that only after being supervised by the Church were the designs handed over for the weavers to work from.

This is not to say that artistic representations of the same scene always agree in detail. In some Resurrection or 'Doom' sculptures, portrayals of the risen dead are not always consistent. At Notre Dame in Paris they are shown clothed, at Basle Cathedral on the north portal they appear to be hastily dressing, while at Bourges the saved appear before God's throne fully arrayed—the damned are naked. Yet, just as theologians differed on various points, so, it seems, artists followed the instructions given at the particular church where they were working.

Legends of the saints also had a way of becoming changed and embroidered through the years. The case of St Nicholas, Bishop of Myra, illustrates this. He was adopted as the patron saint of children, though his chief claim to fame was that he had converted and baptised hundreds of pagans in Asia Minor. He was usually portrayed, therefore, in early times, as standing by a baptismal font in which were three naked pagans. During the centuries the font was mistaken for a pickling tub, and a legend developed that three children had been placed in it after being murdered by the host of an inn in which St Nicholas passed the night. Discovering the dismembered children, the saint blessed them and restored them to life. This strangely distorted tale is illustrated in the sixteenth-century stained glass of Beauvais Cathedral.

Individual artists also defied the conservatism of the Church and made changes in traditional forms. But the case of Tidemann, a German carver, shows how seriously the matter of ecclesiastic discipline was taken by the Church authorities. In 1306 Tidemann had made a crucifix for a London church which was 'wrongly carved, with a cross piece quite contrary to the true representation of the cross . . . to which the indiscreet populace flock in crowds, as to a true crucifix, which it certainly is not, whence we see great peril for their souls'. The bishop ordered that Tidemann must surrender the bond for £23 which the rector of the church had given him. He also had to carry away the crucifix, secretly and without scandal, before dawn or after dark, into some other diocese. Meantime he must take a solemn oath that henceforth he would neither offer, nor make for sale, such 'deformed crucifixes in our diocese of London'.

Perhaps an earlier case brought against certain Spanish craftsmen in the late thirteenth century may explain this matter of 'deformed crucifixes'. Bishop Tuy accused the men of

painting or carving ill-shapen images of saints in order that by gazing on them the devotion of Christian folk may be turned to loathing. In derision and scorn of Christ's cross, they carve images of Our Lord with one foot laid over the other, so that both are pierced by a single nail, thus striving to annul men's faith in the Holy Cross, and the traditions of the sainted Fathers, by super-inducing these novelties.

In the earliest crucifixes the figure was draped and the feet separately nailed. Only during the thirteenth

72 An eleventh-century crucifix

century did it gradually become customary to omit draperies and portray the ankles crossed, whereby one nail could be used instead of two. But so important was tradition that artists who tried to introduce 'novelties' were often at first penalised, as was Tidemann. Nevertheless, tradition did change from century to century. Varying representations of the Nativity demonstrate this. In tenth-to-twelfth-century manuscripts, the Holy Babe is shown, not in Mary's arms, not even in a manger or a crib, but lying on an altar. Above Him burns an altar lamp, hung between two curtains. The scene is not a stable, but a church. Mary lies below, turning away as she contemplates the fate of her son, while Joseph stands, sharing her sorrow. This symbolism is designed to teach that, from the moment of birth, Jesus is the sacrificial victim. To make the symbolism clearer the figure of Christ on the cross is sometimes shown above the Babe on the altar. The cult of the Virgin, which developed so strongly during the late twelfth and the thirteenth centuries, gradually affected this sterner aspect of the Nativity. It is not until this later period that Mary was depicted with the Babe in her arms or gazing down at Him with infinite love.

The portrayal of current 'scientific' beliefs in

churches are taken mainly from the Besti-aries—books of myth and fable about animals and plants, with commentaries giving symbolic interpretations which illustrate some aspect of the Christian faith. One example is found on a capital from Troyes (now in the Louvre, Paris) on which the 'peredexion' tree is shown. Birds perch in its branches, while beneath two dragons lie in wait. The tree is described in the medieval Bestiaries as having such sweet fruit that

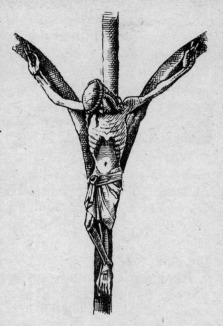

73   A fourteenth-century plague cross

doves are attracted to settle in its branches. The shadow of the tree is, however, fatal to dragons. This the birds know, so that as long as they shelter on the shaded side they are safe. Here, the peredexion symbolises the tree of life, the birds are souls nourished by its fruit, while its shadow is fatal to the forces of evil.

The everyday life of the worker is also a favourite subject for the artist. Calendars, with the zodiacal sign for the month and the appropriate activity being enacted below it, are found in the sculptures and stained glass of many cathedrals.

Martianus Capella, an African grammarian of the fifth century, in his book on the arts which was long popular in the Middle Ages, symbolised the various subjects of the *trivium* and the *quadrivium* as beautiful women. Early personalisations of the Seven Arts are found in many cathedrals, among them Music is seen on a window at Laon, while in the old west porch at Chartres the Seven are shown through sculptures, accompanied by figures who perhaps represent the inventor of each art. At Florence, frescoes in the Spanish Chapel in Santa Maria Novella portray the same subject.

Works of art of a purely historical character are not found as frequently in the cathedrals as those which illustrate biblical events. The famous Charlemagne window at Chartres, though portraying actual as well as symbolic scenes, is primarily intended to record victories of the Faith and the Church gained through the agency of the emperor.

Religious enthusiasm was the chief inspiration of most medieval art. The lives and work of those builders and artists who have left any record of their aim and interests demonstrate this. One of these craftsmen was Airardus, a monk, who was possibly master of works of the new church of Saint-Denis, erected by the Frankish Abbot Fulrad, and consecrated by Charlemagne in 775. Airardus is probably the earliest artist-builder of whom we have a likeness. He made the bronze doors for the main entrance of the Romanesque church which was later altered by Abbot Suger. The doors (since destroyed) had Airardus' portrait engraved on them, with a couplet in Latin below:

This work, Airardus, trusting in the grace, O St Denis,
With humble heart, he herewith offers now to thee.

In the eighth-century engraving—preserved only by a later copy—Airardus appeared as many monkish builders and artists must have done, in the ankle-length working-robe of a Benedictine monk. His plump face was placid and serene; yet, in spite of the great honour accorded him, of being commemorated on the chief door of a royal Carolingian church, his attitude was full of diffidence as he offered his work to the saint.

Two other Carolingian portraits of a donor, and perhaps of the monk architect of the church, are found on the walls of the oratory of San Benedetto at Malles in the Tyrol. On the left a nobleman stands bareheaded holding his sword as a cross, on the right a monk with ardent face holds the model of the church shown without its present tower. This has been acclaimed as one of the most beautiful portraits of the Carolingian Age.

Einhard, Charlemagne's secretary, was also an architect. A vivid contemporary word-portrait brings him before us as 'little Nard, who runs ceaselessly to and fro like a tiny ant, burdened by books or heavy packages'. Well liked by all in the scholastic and courtly circles surrounding Charlemagne, Einhard was also a gifted worker in precious metals as a young man. He probably made the miniature triumphal arch in silver which he gave to the monastery of St Servais at Maastricht of which he was lay abbot. If it is true that 'art is man's thought expressed in his handiwork', certainly many of the buildings and smaller works of art around the year 800 express the enthusiasm for the monuments of Christian Rome which was a characteristic of this time. Charlemagne's coronation by the Pope in Rome as 'the most serene Augustus, governing the Roman Empire' had stimulated the interest of his subjects in the former Roman Empire. It was no mere whim which caused Einhard to decorate his triumphal arch—made as the stand for a cross—not only with figures of Christ, but also with warriors of Antiquity and two emperors as well.

Buildings also mirrored this conscious pride in belonging to a renewed Roman Empire. Abbot Ricbod (*d*. 804), or perhaps his successor, built a charming new

74   Gateway at Lorsch

gateway to the monastery church at Lorsch, south of Mainz in Germany. This incorporates many classical details, although itself unclassical in style. Nevertheless, its inspiration is the Arch of Constantine in Rome.

From the earliest times the building of churches was the result of intense enthusiasm on the part of patrons, one of the greatest of these being Charlemagne himself. Often it was the desire of abbots to provide a fitting shrine and setting for the relics of the saints which led to the rebuilding of a church. Angilbert, one of Charlemagne's most brilliant courtiers, and the lover of one of his strictly guarded daughters, was impelled, partly in token of contrition for his sins, partly to house relics of saints, to build—under Charlemagne's patronage—the church of the monastery of Centula (Saint Riquier) of which he had been made abbot. Angilbert, a passionate lover of beauty, acquired for his church a fabulous collection of treasures, including almost a hundred relics of martyrs, confessors and virgins whose altars were given a prominent position in the new church. Before them, Angilbert and his monks performed each day an elaborate liturgy. For a belief in the aid of the saints, trust in the Christian

Faith as a whole, and loyalty to comrades and one's secular lord, were three of the strongest bonds which gave cohesion to medieval society.

By the late twelfth century, however, Gothic art was taking the place of Romanesque and some of its master-builders, artists and patrons have left manuscripts and books which throw an illuminating light on their work and ideas. Bishop Suger, who largely rebuilt the Romanesque church of St Denis and has left detailed accounts of his work, can be described as one of the first patrons of Gothic art. Between him and the master-masons, artists and craftsmen he employed, there was the closest liaison. As soon as he became abbot, Suger began raising funds for rebuilding and redecorating the church. To make the basilica the most resplendent in the western world became the chief aim of the abbot's life. It is true Suger was not without vanity. His name appears on most of the inscriptions recording the work done on the church:

> For the splendour of the church that has fostered and exalted him, Suger has laboured for the splendour of the church;

and again, on one of the lintels:

> Receive, O stern judge, the prayers of Thy Suger,
> Grant that I be mercifully numbered among Thy own sheep.

Nevertheless, Suger did not spare himself bodily anxiety and fatigue to put his ideals into practice. When long beams were needed to roof the new western portion of the church, no suitable timbers could be found on the abbey estates.

> But on a certain night [he tells us] when I had returned from celebrating Matins, I began to think in bed that I myself should go through all the forests

in these parts. . . . So, hurrying in the early morning, we hastened with our carpenters, and with the measurement of the beams, to the forest called Iveline. [Then, summoning] the keepers of our own forests, as well as those who knew about other woods, we questioned them under oath, whether we could find there, no matter with how much trouble, any timbers of that measure. At this they smiled— indeed they would have laughed at us if they had dared. Almost pityingly they declared nothing of the kind could be found in the entire region.

Suger, however, although nearing 60, insisted on searching the forests, and with the others he struggled 'through the thickets and dense, thorny tangles', and by the ninth hour the 12 necessary timbers had been found and marked. This is typical of the man always to take an active share in the planning and building of the church. He tells us that he himself selected indi- vidual craftsmen, that he insisted on the placing of a mosaic against the wishes of others, and that the iconography of window designs, of crucifixes and altar paintings were designed by him. The rose window in his church started a fashion that was to become famous in Gothic architecture. His death in 1151 marked the passing of a man indomitable to the end, one who had set himself a great task and had fulfilled it. 'He was not loath to die, because he had enjoyed to live. He departed willingly . . . for he did not hold that a good man should leave like one that is ejected, one who is thrown out against his will.'

Another famous manuscript—*On Diverse Arts*—was left by Theophilus, the pseudonym of Roger of Hel- mershausen, who was a monk, skilled in many arts, but particularly in metalwork. The monastery of Helmers- hausen, in the diocese of Paderborn, was, in the twelfth century, one of the most important art centres of north-west Germany. It produced works of art for great princes and bishops, and had a wide reputation for the excellence of its metalwork and the beauty of its illuminated manuscripts, as well as for its wall paintings and stained glass. Theophilus first tells us that the mainspring of his artistic work was the love of God. I have laboured, he writes,

> out of no love for human praise, or for greed of temporal gain, nor have I retained anything precious or rare, nor kept silent about something reserved especially for myself from malice or envy, but that to increase the honour and glory of His name, I have ministered to the needs of the many and have had regard to their advantage.

In the Preface to the last part of his book, he breaks out into panegyric about church decoration:

> Animated, dearest son, by these supporting virtues, you have approached the House of God with confidence and have adorned it with so much beauty; you have embellished the ceilings and walls with varied work in different colours, and have, in some measure, shown to beholders the paradise of God, glowing with varied flowers, verdant with herbs and foliage, and cherishing with crowns of varying merit the souls of the saints. You have given them cause to praise the Creator in the creature, and proclaim Him wonderful in His works. For the human eye is not able to consider on what work first to fix its gaze; if it beholds the ceilings, they glow like brocades; if they consider the walls, they are a kind of paradise; if it regards the profusion of light from the windows, it marvels at the inestimable beauty of the glass and the infinitely rich and varied workman-

ship. If perchance the faithful soul observes the
representation of the Lord's Passion, it stung with
compassion. . . . If it beholds how great are the joys
of heaven, how great the torments in the eternal
flames, it is animated by the hope of its good deeds,
and is shaken with fear by reflection on its sins.

The main part of the monk's book, is, however, above
all, practical. Through it we are enabled to see the life
of the lay and monkish craftsmen in a great monastery
devoted to the production of works of art. We see the
workshops and work-furnaces of the metal-workers and
their tools—bellows, anvils, hammers and crucibles;
we learn how to construct kilns for making stained
glass, what ingredients are necessary and the method of
mixing them; we are told in detail how to mingle
colours to gain different effects in portraiture, wall-
painting and the illumination of books; and about the
making of sacred vessels in gold and silver and niello
work, as well as about the art of enamelling and the
setting of gems. As if this were not enough, Theophilus
gives a detailed description for constructing an organ, as
well as for the founding of bells. One, at least, of the
works of art made by the monk-artist himself is preserved in the cathedral treasury of Paderborn. It is a
costly portable altar made about 1100 for Bishop
Henry of Paderborn, a great patron of the arts (*78*).
Another manuscript left by a medieval artist is the
Album of Villars de Honnecourt, a famous thirteenth-
century master-builder. In the Middle Ages, architects,
as we know them, did not exist. Stone buildings were
erected under the supervision of a master-mason,
wooden buildings under that of a master-carpenter.
Master-builders especially were men of versatile
talents and were usually widely travelled. From
Villar's *Album* we can deduce something of his know-

75　A professor and his students
Detail from a fourteenth-century tomb in Pistoia Cathedral

76　St Michael weighs the souls of the dead
Detail of the tympanum of Bourges Cathedral

77   An angel summons the souls of the dead for the Last Judgement
From a French manuscript

ledge of the technique of architecture. One of his sketches shows a rose light constructed with joggle joints. This was necessary to give the extra support needed by the tracery because of the delicacy of the design. It was by these and more complicated developments in engineering skill that French architects invented the flying buttress and discovered the secrets of ogive vaulting, which is supported by intersecting and pointed-arch ribs. By giving additional strength to walls, the flying buttress made possible the insertion of windows with wonderful rose and traceried designs like those at Chartres and Reims. In consequence a Gothic cathedral, in contrast to the small-windowed Romanesque buildings, appeared to be flooded with light, and magical effects were obtained when the sun poured through the jewelled glass with which they were filled.

That aspects of medieval philosophy appealed to Villars is shown by the inclusion in his book of a sketch of the Wheel of Fortune. This illustrates a passage from Boethius, the philosopher whose *On the Consolations of Philosophy*—one of the noblest books of the early Middle Ages—was widely read until the eleventh century. After being a favourite of the Gothic Emperor Theodoric, the philosopher was judicially murdered by him in A.D. 524. Small wonder that Boethius put into Fortune's mouth the words:

> I cause a rapid wheel to turn. I love to raise the fallen and abase the proud. Mount then, if thou wilt, but on condition that thou dost not wax indignant when the law which presides at my Games, demands that thou shalt descend.

Fortune's wheel is sculptured on the south rose window at Amiens, on the north porch of St Etienne at Beauvais and in the porch of the cathedral at Basle. It

was a favourite subject with miniaturists and in *Somme
le Roi*, a medieval book, it is stated: 'In these cathedral
churches and royal abbeys, is Dame Fortune who turns
topsy-turvy faster than a windmill.'

Villars also mentions master-craftsmen who worked
and argued and drank with him, then wandered off to
distant lands where they lie buried, or rest beneath
some cloister pavement nearer home, but through their
wanderings and discussions new styles and ideas were
carried from one part of Europe to another. Hugh
Libergier—a contemporary of Villars—helped to build
the church of St Nicaise in Reims. He is depicted on his
tombstone in Reims Cathedral as a stately figure in his
master's cap and gown. In his right hand he holds his
measuring rod, in his left the model of St Nicaise, while
his square and compasses are shown below. Villars
spent considerable time in Reims making sketches of
the cathedral so that it is most likely that he and Hugh
discussed mutual problems together. Villars certainly
conferred with Pierre de Corbie, his fellow-architect,
on how to construct vaults in a presbytery that had
alternate square and round chapels. How to make a
wheel turn of its own accord, or how to construct a
cross-bow that could not miss its mark, or the method of
'making the eagle on the lectern turn its head towards
the deacon when he reads the Gospel at Mass' were all
subjects of interest to these medieval architects. We
see Villars also eagerly writing down the recipe made of
'quicklime and orpiment' which a fellow-mason gave
him. The recipe so carefully preserved for over 600 years
is 'for removing superfluous hairs'.

Another of Villars' contemporaries—but socially of
a higher status—was Eudes de Montreuil, a favourite
master mason of St Louis, who accompanied the king on
his Crusade and built the towers of Jaffa. Thevet in
1584 included Eudes' portrait among his illustrious

Frenchmen because 'he concerned himself with things mechanical, and was not of those who puff themselves up. Michael Angelo, industrious as he was, would not have done as much work in 60 years as Eudes in 20.'

Perhaps hearing that Eudes had gone on Crusade with the king, Villars was inspired to draw his working model of a mangonel, for siege operations. For Villars also 'concerned himself with things mechanical'. Nevertheless the modern verdict on Villars' mathematical capabilities is that they 'illustrate the extreme poverty of the art of measuring heights and distances in the thirteenth century'. No doubt this explains the frequency with which medieval towers collapsed. Yet nothing can detract from the wonder and impressive beauty of those which still stand. Villars himself especially admired the tower of Laon which had been recently erected. 'I have been in many countries, but in no place have I seen a tower to equal it.' His sketch shows the heads of sculptured oxen peering from the base of the tower between the pillars. A charming legend centres round these animals. Once, one of a team of oxen fell exhausted as it helped to drag a heavy load of stone uphill for the building of Laon Cathedral. The wagoner was in despair, when, to his surprise he saw another ox approaching. It offered itself to be yoked in place of the fallen animal. After delivering the stone, the wagoner found that the unknown ox had disappeared. In remembrance of this miracle and in gratitude to all the beasts that had helped to raise the cathedral the sculptor placed the oxen on the tower.

Whatever the truth of the legend, it demonstrates a medieval in-

78   Portable altar made by Roger of Helmershausen

79 Villars de Honnecourt's
sketch for Laon cathedral

terest in animals. Man-
uscripts abound in ref-
erences to the well-
loved cats of monks.
Villars' drawings in-
clude a cat, a bear, a
swan, a pair of perching
parrots and a lion, with
the note, 'Mark well,
this lion is counterfeited
from life!' His carefully
drawn shell of a snail,
of a grasshopper, a fly, a
dragonfly and a lobster,
testify to his keen ob-
servation. But this is
true of countless ob-
scure masons. Medieval
cathedrals contain
many life-like studies
of flowers and plants.
The plantain, butter-
cup, ferns, clover, celandines, cress, snapdragons and
many others decorating friezes and capitals, all testify
to that nostalgic love of wild flowers which the country-
bred seldom lose, since they recall the sun-filled spring
and summer days of childhood.

Maybe the arum leaf and lily, used in medieval
times for incantations and witchcraft, were chosen by
simple craftsmen as models so that, by being placed in a
Christian building, they would be exorcised of their
evil powers. The gargoyles, terrifying beasts, creatures
half-men, half-animal, are echoes, no doubt, of fireside
tales told on winter nights. Indeed Gothic architecture
holds much of magic and enchantment. To men previously accustomed to the solid, down-to-earth quali-

ties of Romanesque buildings, the graceful pillars and arches, the flying buttresses, the unbelievable delicacy of traceries in stone, the beauty of rose windows with their jewel-like stained glass and of slender pinnacles soaring towards the sky must have appeared miraculous even to their makers. This grace and airiness, allied to originality in technique and design, seems all the more inexplicable when we recall that, in addition to the discipline of choice imposed by the Church, medieval masons had strict rules imposed upon them by their guild. Nevertheless it had always been more difficult to impose regulations upon masons than upon other guild members. Even as late as 1356 the authorities complained that in London 'masons were not regulated in due manner by the government of folks of their trade in such forms as other trades are'. It was therefore more difficult to penalise them. Masons were 'here today and gone tomorrow' by the very nature of their craft. In 1380, Wyclif in England complained that 'men of subtle crafts, as freemasons and others, conspire together to refuse statutory wages and to insist upon a rise', and this was equally true throughout Europe for masons, particularly after the Black Death.

In Germany, masons do not seem to have organised themselves into chapters, so that scattered groups could be controlled, until the early fifteenth century. Then, in 1456, German masons boycotted one—Jodochus Tauchen—because

> they doubted whether he had properly satisfied all conditions of the mason's customs, which were then kept more strictly than nowadays; they doubted whether he had rightly learned his craft, and had proved his capacity for mastership publicly before the guild. Therefore they would allow none of the

apprentices to work with Jodochus, who had learned in their own lodges.

Jodochus had carved a ciborium, the receptacle in which the consecrated wafer was kept. This can still be seen in the 'Elizabeth Church' at Breslau with Tauchen's mark upon it. It is a graceful example of Gothic work but apparently it met with disapproval from his guild. Masters who were already in a guild were beginning to make the standard for a 'masterpiece' so high and the cost of making it so extortionate that it was increasingly difficult for new applicants to gain entrance to the guild. In addition there were heavy fees to pay the craft court when such a masterpiece was presented, and a sumptuous banquet to provide for existing members when successful. Further fees were payable to the municipality of the town where the mason lived. At guild banquets or at formal business meetings after which a feast was often held, the standard of behaviour was evidently high. Rules of etiquette were formulated in English and German guild statutes:

> *Good manners maketh a man . . .*
> *Look that thine hands be clean*
> *And that thy knife be sharp and keen . . .*
> *If thou sit by a worthier man*
>
> *Than thyself art one,*
> *Suffer him first to touch the meat.*
> *In chamber among ladies bright,*
> *Hold thy tongue and spend thy sight.*

Master-masons were those who had attained the highest positions in their craft. But there were many grades, determined by both social status and economic position. Many masons began life as quarry workers, then, if they showed proficiency, they might be employed as the servant or labourer of a trained mason.

At Ely in 1359–60 John Linne was the servant of John Stubbard, *cementarius* or mason. In 1436, a John Wade of Colchester, mason, was granted 'board in the County Hall for himself as a gentleman and for his servant as a yeoman'. The general run of workers connected with building included hewers, layers, wallers, marblers, paviors and image-makers, all with different rates of pay. Some are described as 'diggers and common workmen'. These levelled the ground, made and carried mortar, wheeled stones in barrows to the masons' workshops—or 'lodges', as they were called— and dug and laid foundations. There were, in addition, lime-burners, tool-carriers, hod-bearers, and men for working pulleys similar to those still found in the lofts of cathedrals and abbey churches. Most of these lowly workers would probably be local men who were often impressed for any large undertaking such as the building of a church, castle or stone bridge.

But trained masons travelled long distances to get employment, and it may be due to the fact that a man had gained freedom from his guild to work and travel where he liked, that he was named a 'free-mason'. The term may be derived, however, from the ability of some craftsmen to work in freestone from which the delicate traceries and carvings for windows and capitals were fashioned. Still another possible derivation of the word is from the Irish custom whereby a 'skilled craftsman of unfree race became by virtue of his craft a free man'. The term does not seem to signify that a freemason could claim exemption from impressment. The punishment for refusal to work where the king ordered was imprisonment; ecclesiastical and lay builders alike were liable to be impressed when any king or ruler needed to have a building erected in haste.

One or more lodges, in which masons did some of

80   Carpenters and masons building
Chartres Cathedral

their work, were erected on building sites. They seem to have taken meals and also their midday siesta in the lodge. Sometimes a special loft above the workshop was erected for eating and resting in, and a lodge was large enough to accommodate 14–20 masons. Hotels or dwelling-houses, quite separate from lodges, were usually provided for masons working on a large project. Strict rules governed each lodge. On an ecclesiastical building site, the Chapter drew up the regulations, and the master-mason in charge of the lodge swore to their observance. It was he who reported any cases of bad work or insubordination to the clergy who were in charge of the finances and administration of the fabric of the church.

The power of the Chapter over its employees is demonstrated in the case of a master-carpenter—Philippe Viart—who was noted for the excellence of his carving. In 1466, the Chapter of Rouen engaged him to make them a new set of choir stalls. After some time, the Chapter complained that the work was going too slowly. They dismissed Viart's carpenters and took on others. Still they were dissatisfied. Viart was repeatedly warned, and, after five months, dismissed. He, his wife and children had to set out in search of further work. His task was probably not as difficult as that confronting the Cathedral Chapter, for it took them three weeks to recruit fresh carpenters and they had to be drawn from as far afield as Lille, Tournai and Brussels.

It looks as if Viart had been paid, not by time, but 'by the piece', a system that was introduced in the later Middle Ages and was resented by the workers. The Chapter of Rouen obviously thought that Viart and his men were not making enough choir stalls in a given time. Judging by the high price of £20 given to Tidemann in 1306 for his crucifix, a skilled craftsman could demand a high price for his work.

But by the fifteenth century the zenith of Gothic art was passed. Victor Hugo's dictum, 'The Gothic sun set behind the colossal press at Mainz', states one reason for the eclipse. For, by 1500, at least 40 printing presses were turning out books in Germany, France, Italy, the Netherlands and England. Religious inspiration no longer spurred the artist to perfection as in the twelfth and thirteenth centuries. The cathedral's work of teaching through the plastic arts was also ending. Christianity's new task was to learn to function as an inward force.

9

DOCTORS AND PATIENTS

I insist that those who treat the health of body of the
brethren . . . must serve with honest study to aid the
sick as becomes their knowledge of medicine. . . .
Learn therefore the nature of herbs, and seek to
know how to combine the various kinds for human
health; do not, however, entirely place your hope on
herbs. Since medicine has been created by God, and
since it is He who restores health, turn to Him. Do all
that you do in word or deed in the name of the Lord
Jesus. . . . If you cannot read Greek, then read the
translations of Dioscorides which accurately describe the herbs of the field. Then read translations of
Hippocrates, Galen and Aurelius Celsus and other
medical works which, by God's help, I have provided
for you in my library.

FROM these directions, put forward by Cassiodorus
(*d.* 575) the friend of St Benedict, regarding the treatment of illness, it can be seen that religion was as
dominating an influence in the realm of medieval
medicine as it was in that of art. For traditional knowledge of herbal medicine, based on the works of Greek
and Roman physicians was not enough for this pious
and learned founder of a Calabrian monastery.
Christian faith, as well as the provision of hospitals,
were needed in addition to effect a cure.

It was again monks who kept alive medical, as indeed

every other form of knowledge, during the centuries of barbarism that succeeded the fall of Rome. This care for the ailing was at first mainly directed towards the monks themselves and towards the lay brethren within the monastery. No doubt workers on monastic estates were also tended, when they fell sick. But the masses would have to depend for treatment during illness on their womenfolk, or on those whom Boccaccio in the fourteenth century referred to as 'quacks and women pretenders'.

Nobles and kings had their own physicians who, except perhaps in Italy, were clerics. Charlemagne often ignored the advice of his doctors who were particularly unpopular when they recommended him in later life to change from eating roast meat, which he loved, to stews which he did not. He also disliked fasting and considered that the practice did him harm. Nevertheless diet was considered important by many doctors throughout the Middle Ages. In this earlier period, Anthimus, Greek physician of Theodoric the Great who ruled from Ravenna, declared 'Man's health depends on a proper diet. Above all, moderation is necessary.' He, like Charlemagne's doctors, believed that fasting was beneficial to health. Anthimus' books on medicine were in use up to the ninth and tenth centuries.

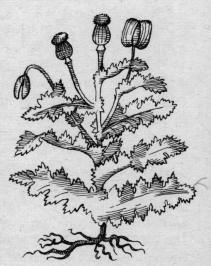

81   Poppy illustrated in a herbal

But in the early cen-

turies the chronicles and records recount many cures
through the agency of the Virgin, of saintly bishops still
alive or of saints who from their tombs and through their
relics performed miracles of healing, and sound a note
of scorn and intolerance for any form of human medicine. We are told of Eustachia, Bishop Gregory of
Tour's niece, who in the sixth century devoted herself
to the sick and ailing. The Bishop describes how a certain woman was afflicted by demons who caused her
tongue to be paralysed:

> The people tried an appliance of herbs and verbal
> incantations; but were unable by medical skill to
> allay the malady. . . . Our daughter [Eustachia],
> coming to the sick woman and seeing her with the
> foolish herb dressing, poured oil from the Holy
> Sepulchre into her mouth, with the result that the
> sick woman began to convalesce.

Stories of miraculous cures by the Virgin are
numerous. One tells of a man at Nevers suffering from
the *mal des ardents*. This was an epidemic of a cancerous
nature which ravaged northern France in 1128 and
1129. The man, despairing of cure, had his foot ampu-
tated. After praying in the cathedral he fell asleep and
woke to find his foot had been restored by the Virgin,
so that he walked away on his two feet.

Alongside this widespread belief in the healing power
of Christian faith, the use of pagan incantations and
practices highly tinged with sorcery continued. These
were forbidden by the Church but, under the cover of
the sign of the cross or diluted by an admixture of
Christian names and phrases, pagan practices persisted.
Herb-gatherers, busily plucking flowers or digging
roots under the influence of an appropriate planet,
would be heard to mutter, 'Holy Goddess Earth, parent
of Nature, the Great Mother . . . come to me with thy

healing powers and grant favourable issue to whatsoever I shall make from these herbs and plants. . . . I beseech thee that thy gifts shall make those who take them, whole.' Astrology was regarded as a necessary adjunct to the practice of medicine throughout the Middle Ages, even by the most scientifically minded. There were lucky and unlucky days for blood-letting. One of the first enquiries a doctor made was to ask his patient what star he was born under, as certain remedies were associated with certain planets. Even then it was essential to drink the medicine only when the moon was in a favourable position.

Most cures for simple illnesses were herbal, though these were often combined with most offensive substances—urine, animal excretions, powdered earthworms and the like. A great many prescriptions, including herbs, are found in the writings of medieval leeches and doctors of the early period:

> For headache, take root of peony mixed with oil of roses. Soak linen with the mixture and apply to where the pain is.
> For toothache, mix vinegar, oil and sulphur and put in the mouth of the sufferer.

A less attractive treatment was:

> to take a candle of mutton fat mingled with the seed of sea holly; burn the candle as close to the tooth as possible, holding a basin of cold water underneath. Worms gnawing the tooth will fall into the water to escape the heat of the candle.

Abbot Strabo of Reichenau contrived in the ninth century to combine his interest in medicine with enthusiasm for his herb garden. He describes how the nettles were everywhere when he began to dig. But he persevered and soon had:

sage and rue and southernwood, poppy and penny-
royal, mint and parsley and radishes, and, for love's
sake only, gladioli and lilies and roses, even though
only plain German roses, no Tyrian purple nor the
scarlet splendour of France.

As for the herbs themselves, Strabo put his prescriptions and their uses into easily remembered verse in
his *Hortulus*. One of these, referring to an antidote for
poisonous aconite, gives us an example of his delightful
humour:

> *If your step-mother, driven by spite,*
> *Secretes in your food under cover of night*
> *An aconite pill, then is filled with delight*
> *When next morning she sees you turn green.*
> *Care naught for her spells! It soon will be seen*
> *That your health is restored, as you sip drop by drop*
> *A cup of my herbs, and all pain they will stop.*

Urine analysis was another method used for the
diagnosis of disease. Notker, in the ninth century, a
monk of the famous monastery of St Gall, 'performed
wonders of healing that were unbelievable by this
method'. When the Duke of Bavaria became his
patient, the nobleman substituted the urine of a
pregnant woman for his own, in order to test Notker.
After his anslysis, the monk turned to the Duke and
said, 'God is about to perform a miracle. Within 30
days, the Duke will give birth to a child.' Needless to
say, Notker was appointed as the ducal physician.
Tables were drawn up during the Middle Ages which
showed the significance of the colour of urine for the
diagnosis of disease, and it was a fairly common sight
to see a servant carrying along the street a flask containing a sample of urine in its specially shaped basket,
on its way for examination by a physician.

Were all doctors at this period, then, clerics like Notker? Not in Italy, where laymen seem to have practised medicine from classical times. Salerno, on its beautiful and sheltered bay, had long been a health resort and by the ninth century was a flourishing medical cen-

82 A doctor drops the urine glass indicating the patient's likely death

tre. Near by was the Benedictine monastery of Monte Cassino whose Abbot was keenly interested in medicine and who had compiled two medical works. Most important perhaps, Salerno was in that part of Italy which had once been colonised by Greece, so that Greek was still spoken there, making it possible to make use of medical manuscripts which remained in the Benedictine library—salvage from the wreck of the ancient world.

By the eleventh century the Salernitan school was developing into the most important university in Europe for the training of physicians. It was there laid down that three years' of study in the liberal arts was to be followed by four years' medical study, with a final year of practical work under a qualified physician. If the student intended to practise surgery, a year's study of anatomy was compulsory.

One of the most famous teachers at Salerno was Constantinus Africanus, who was born in Carthage early in the eleventh century. He knew Arabic but not Greek, and took to Salerno Arabian books and a thorough knowledge of Arabian medicine. Duke Robert of Salerno invited Constantine to become his physician, but the African spent a great deal of his time translating—not always accurately—the medical works of Hippocrates, Galen and Celsus, as well as the writings of the Moorish physician Avicenna from Arabic into Latin. It was not until the later Renaissance that dependable translations of classical writers were made. A popular book containing rhymed commonsense maxims for health was also compiled at Salerno:

> *If you would health and vigour keep,*
> *Shun care and anger ere you sleep.*
> *All heavy fare and wine disdain,*
> *From noonday slumber, too, refrain.*
> *Each day to walk awhile you should*
> *For this will work you naught but good.*
> *The urgent calls of Nature heed.*
> *These rules obey and you will find,*
> *Long life is yours and tranquil mind.*

One of the most widely known of the Salernitan rules for health is still applicable today:

> *Use three physicians still—first Dr Quiet*
> *Next Dr Merryman and third Dr Diet.*

Another medical theory firmly believed in for many centuries was stated in verse:

> *Four Humours reign within our body wholly*
> *And these compared to four elements*
> *The Sanguine, Cholar, Phlegm and Melancholy.*

A vivid picture of an eleventh-century doctor can be gained by reading the Salernitan *Instruction for the Physician Himself*. We see him on his way with the messenger who has summoned him to visit a patient. The *instruction* advised him to question the servant closely as to the exact nature and circumstances of his master's illness:

Then, if not able to make a positive diagnosis after examining the patient's pulse and urine, he will at least excite astonishment by his accurate knowledge of the symptoms of the disease, and so win his confidence. The fingers should also be kept on the pulse, until at least the hundredth beat, to judge its character. Those standing round will be all the more impressed by the delay. On entering the house the physician should not appear too haughty, but greet with kindly, modest demeanour those present. Then, after seating himself by the sick man he should accept the drink offered, and proceed to put the patient at his ease before examining him.

The acquisition of a good bedside manner was regarded as of great importance:

Let the physician have clean hands and well shapen nails, cleansed from all blackness and filth. Let him also learn good proverbs pertaining to his craft in comforting patients. Also it speedeth if a doctor can talk of good tales to make his patient laugh for they induce a light heart to the sick man.

As regards fees, a surgeon of 1380 who specialised in the treatment of *fistula* (ulcer) tells us:

For the cure of *fistula*, when it is curable, ask a well-to-do man a hundred marks or £40 with a supply of robes and a yearly fee of 100s. for life. . . . From a poorer man take no less than 100s. For never in my life took I less for curing that sickness.

After Salerno, Montpellier in southern France won fame for the excellence of its medical school. Already well known by the eleventh century, it probably owed much to its proximity to Spain and consequent access to Greek medical knowledge through transla-

83   The Humours, Melancholy and Phlegm

tions by Jewish and Moslem physicians. At Montpellier
it was found that smallpox patients, if wrapped in red
cloth with red hangings placed around their bed,
rapidly improved and recovery was possible without
pockmarks being left. This treatment is suggestive of
the Finson's red-light cure of modern times. Both
Montpellier and Salerno had well-run hospitals early
in their history. Hospitals were Christian in origin, and
the fourth-century Emperor Julian, the Apostate
declared, 'Now we can see what makes these Christians
such powerful enemies of our gods; it is the brotherly
love which they manifest towards strangers, the sick
and the poor.' He therefore advocated the setting up of
rival hospitals run by pagans.

St Benedict's Rule laid down that every monastery
must have a hospital. But, as we have seen, these were
mainly for the monks and lay brethren. If all monastic
hospitals were as excellent as that planned in the
ninth century for St Gall in Switzerland, they reached a
high standard indeed. On the plan, which may be an
ideal one never actually executed, separate quarters
were provided for the several physicians and the
infirmary was segregated from other buildings, with its

84   The Humours, Sanguine and Choler

own separate chapel and open courtyard. There were
heated and unheated rooms, a fine dormitory and
refectory, kitchens, baths and many toilets. Special
rooms were reserved for serious cases, and for blood-
letting and purging. A pharmacy, dispensary and herb
garden were also provided.

But it was during the twelfth and thirteenth centuries
that a sudden increase in the work of Christian charity
for the poor and sick took place. Innocent III, who
inaugurated the Fourth Crusade in 1204, built the
Hospital of the Holy Spirit in Rome, following the plan
of the hospital which Guy de Montpellier had built in
his native town. The increase in the tempo of hospital
and leprosary building during these centuries seems
to correspond to the monastic and papal reform movements then taking place, and with the accompanying
upsurge of intense religious feeling. In some places it was
the growth of the independence and power of the towns
which resulted in a spate of endowments for new chari-
ties and hospitals.

Very few of the hospitals and leprosaries at this time
were mere converted houses, but were specially built.
When, in the mid-thirteenth century, Toulouse, for

instance, had a population of about 25,000, 7 leprosaries and 12 hospitals existed in the town. The local monasteries in addition had infirmaries for their monks, with separate ones for the lay brothers, and gate services for the poor. The leprosaries were rather small, only two having chapels attached. Each of these seemed to have had about 10 inmates, so that in all some 70 institutional lepers were being cared for. The hospitals in Toulouse varied considerably in size. In 1243 one had 56 beds. Some were smaller with only 13 residents. Much care and thought went into the planning of these buildings. The Hospital of the Holy Ghost at Lübeck, built in the thirteenth century, had excellent features: high ceilings, large windows and running water in the vicinity which, directed into the monastic drains and piping system, provided for the disposal of sewage and waste, as well as for a constant supply of water. In the Hôtel Dieu at Beaune (which still exists), each patient's bed has its original red hangings, while in the hospital at Tonerre there were panelled partitions between beds, thus ensuring privacy.

Perhaps the most dreaded medieval diseases were St Anthony's Fire, leprosy and bubonic plague. St Anthony's Fire, or erysipelas, was caused through eating corrupt rye bread, while the spread of leprosy may have been increased among the poor by their consumption of putrid fish and meat: 'When flesh or fish is found to be unclean,' states one University regulation, 'let it be given to the hospital of St John.' Nevertheless, the fact that lepers were segregated in special leprosaries and forbidden to mix with healthy members of the population proves that the infectious nature of some diseases was recognised in these early centuries.

As for the Black Death, as it was later called, the

85   A wife makes a medicinal drink for her sick husband
From a late fourteenth-century English manuscript

86   The Polos leaving Venice for their travels to the Far East
*From ' The travels of Marco Polo, or the Book of the Grand Khan', written
in 1338*

horror of this pestilence is mirrored in every European chronicle of the period. Once this dread disease had entered a town or country, ordered life was overthrown more drastically than it had been in the past by attacks of Norse or Saracens. They, at least, after they had struck, usually went away, and from their danger it was possible to flee. But not from the Black Death.

> Whenever one or two people died in any house, at once, or at least in a short space of time, the rest of the household were carried off. So much so, that very often in one home ten or more ended their lives together, and in many houses, the dogs and even cats died. Hence no one, whether rich or poor, was secure, but everyone, from day to day, waited on the will of the Lord.

So writes the chronicler of Tournai. But everywhere it was the same. The disease is thought to have started in China and its cause was not discovered until the nineteenth century. The plague—primarily a disease of rats and other rodents—is spread by infected fleas which, by biting a man, inject the germ into the bloodstream. Guy de Chauliac, the physician of the Pope at Avignon in 1348, and himself a victim who recovered from the plague, diagnosed the disease as of two kinds. The first, which modern physicians recognise as bubonic plague, is characterised by the appearance of buboes or swellings in the groin or armpits. It was this type which de Chauliac contracted and from which it was possible to recover. The second kind, which he recognised as more deadly, was characterised by sharp pains in the chest and the spitting of blood. This—pneumonic plague—was extremely infectious. The third type—the septicaemic form which Guy did not recognise—proved fatal in a few hours since the infection in the bloodstream is so severe there is no time for other symptoms to develop.

We have a contemporary description of the actual arrival of the plague at Messina in Sicily in 1347. We see 12 Genoese trading vessels sailing into the port and tying up at the wharves. Already many of the crew were dying of the terrible pestilence. Those still well went ashore and by their very breath poisoned those who conversed with them. Then,

> seeing what a calamity of sudden death had come to them by the arrival of the Genoese, the people of Messina drove them in all haste from their city and port. But the sickness remained and a terrible mortality ensued. Then the father abandoned the sick son; magistrates and notaries refused to come and make the wills of the dying. The care of those stricken fell to the Friars Minor and members of other orders whose convents were soon emptied of their inhabitants. Corpses were abandoned in empty houses and there was none to give them Christian burial.

Another chronicler tells of the necessity later to bury the dead in great death pits. We see in Provence how rough countrymen, called the *gavoti*, were tempted by large rewards to carry corpses to the grave.

> Daily, some rich man is borne by these ruffians to his burial, without lights, without a friend to follow him. All in the streets fly when his body approaches. Nor do these wretched *gavoti*, strong as they are, escape. Most of them after a time become infected by the contagion and die.

Petrarch, writing from Parma on 19 May 1348, sends a tragic greeting to his brother, the only survivor of a convent of five and thirty.

My brother! My brother! alas what shall I say? Whither shall I turn? On all sides is sorrow, everywhere is fear. I would that I had never been born, or, at least had died before these times. How will posterity believe that there has been a time, without lightnings of heaven or fires of earth, without wars or other visible slaughter, not this or that part of the earth, but well nigh the whole globe has remained without inhabitants? When before has it been seen that houses are left vacant, cities deserted, fields are too small for the dead, and a fearful and universal solitude over the whole earth?

Was nothing then done to try to deal with the plague? The universities themselves were swept almost empty of teachers and students. Nevertheless that of Paris made an attempt to find the causes of the plague so that illness could be combated. It ascribed the origin of the disease to 'the conjunction of three planets on March 20th, 1345. This with other conjunctions and eclipses had caused pernicious corruption of the surrounding air.'

This explanation was followed by writers all over Europe. But in Italy some practical measures were taken. In 1348 those living in Pistoia who wished to visit relatives in Pisa or Lucca would have found the gates of their town all strictly guarded by citizens paid to take their turn at guard duty. Outside the gates merchants, waiting anxiously to sell their linen and woollen goods within the town were turned away, while in the market place inspectors daily examined

87　Burning plague-infected clothes

all food on sale to see that it was fresh. Many funerals passed through the streets, for those were early days and mass burials had not started. 'If a knight, a doctor of laws, or a physician died, trumpeters and criers were allowed to go before the procession to show them the honours that befitted their worth.'

For ordinary people, no bells were to be rung from the churches for fear of frightening the sick, only a limited number of relatives were to attend the funeral to comfort the afflicted.

In 1348 several Italian cities besides Pistoia enforced a sort of quarantine. Lucca was among these. No Genoese or Catalan who had been in any other city or parts of the Romagna could enter the walled town. It was not until 1377, however, that Ragusa made a law that anyone entering the city from a pest region must spend a month in old Ragusa before being admitted to the more modern town. Six years later, Marseilles adopted a 40-day quarantine, so the principle was obviously spreading. Boccaccio, writing from Florence, declared that:

the malady seemed to set at naught both the art of the physician and the virtues of physic. . . . Some people consulted quacks, for there was now a multitude of both men and women who practised without having received the slightest tincture of medical science.

Nevertheless, many physicians laboured unceasingly to treat the sick and try to prevent the spread of the epidemic. One of these was Gentile da Foligno,

the divine prince of physicians. To protect Perugia, he and the venerable college of masters there invoked the divine aid, then drew up directions regarding food and drink, purgation, blood-letting, medicines

88   A doctor ordering medicine from an apothecary

and disinfection. He spent himself caring for the sick until he fell ill from too constant attendance on them. He lived six days and died. I, Francis of Foligno [another doctor] was present at his illness and did not leave him until death.

At last the epidemic burned itself out, to recur less violently throughout the Middle Ages and early modern period. It left a Europe so thinly populated that the social and economic life of the Continent was changed. The mortality at the universities drastically lowered their numbers and many of the most brilliant perished. A moral slackness entered many phases of life, and the hopeful outlook of the thirteenth century, the blaze of intellectual activity of the twelfth, seemed extinguished forever. Instead, throughout Europe, visible in economic, artistic and intellectual decline, gloom and anxiety, and a proneness to dwell on disease

and death settled like a miasma. The reverse side of the
coin shows some efforts being made after the plague to
endow colleges and establish new universities. There
was a growing recognition of students' rights, and in
many countries, owing to the shortage of labour,
peasants were enabled to buy their freedom. But the
overall result of the Black Death was to retard education
and trade and to lead to a general decline in the
fourteenth century which initiated throughout Europe
a period of reduced prosperity.

In the field of surgery both the study of anatomy and
the skill of the surgeon which depended on it, were
practically in abeyance. Physicians, indeed, regarded
surgery as degrading and it was left to barbers to
perform simple operations, like blood-letting. From
the practice of medicine, however, they were jealously
excluded, as a statute of 1271 made by the medical
faculty of Paris, states:

> Since certain manual operators do not know how to
> administer medicines or the relation which medicines
> have to disease, since those matters are reserved
> exclusively to the industry of the skilled physician,
> yet these manual artisans thrusting their sickle into
> alien crops participate in certain cases rashly incur-
> ring sentences of perjuries and excommunications:
> therefore we strictly prohibit that any male or female
> surgeon, apothecary or herbalist presume to exceed
> the limits of their craft . . . so that the surgeon engage
> only in manual practice, the apothecary or herbalist
> only in mixing drugs which are to be administered
> only by masters in medicine or by their licence.

These 'manual operators', the barber surgeons,
working as they did during the period when Crusades
and wars were of frequent occurrence, gained plenty of
practical experience. Nevertheless, without the study of

anatomy through dissection there could be no appreciable advance in the scientific knowledge of surgery.

On the principle that 'the Church abhorreth bloodshed', the ecclesiastical authorities frowned on its practice and a series of laws forbidding clerics to practise surgery was passed. In 1300 Pope Boniface's statute *De Sepultura*, intended to stop the revolting custom of boiling the flesh off Crusaders' bones in order to despatch their bodies home for burial in a less insanitary and bulky form, led indirectly to the virtual cessation of dissection. To procure the corpses even of criminals was by many regarded as a flagrant defiance of the Church's order that the bodies of the dead should not be abused in any way. In Paris, in 1350, the practice of 'manual operation' was forbidden to its bachelors at the university, and even in Italy, where the universities were not so strictly under the domination of the Church, surgery at Bologna University, as late as 1405, was largely theoretical. A student doctor there, interested in the subject of anatomy, must not

> dare to presume to acquire for himself a dead body for dissection unless he has first obtained permission from the rector then in office. . . . Also not more than 20 persons may attend the dissection of a male and not over 30 the dissection of a woman. And he who has seen the dissection of a man cannot attend another the same year. The dissection of a woman he may see once and no more.

This was a most jealously guarded privilege. Permission to view a dissection was given only to a certain number of students chosen from each 'nation' attending the university, no doubt with a view to prevent overcrowding round the table where the dissector and demonstrator stood by the body, while the lecturer held forth from a high rostrum above. He received for his stipend 100 *solidi* Bolognese. We are not told what fees the demonstrator and dissector received, but all expenses incurred were shared equally by the students who attended.

In the fifteenth century, there were many unlicensed women surgeons in Paris. One of these—Peretta Peronne—was, in January 1411, prosecuted by the Master Surgeons of the University. She was brought before the high court in Paris known as the Parlement and, when asked if she knew how to read and what the properties of medicinal herbs were, replied, with feminine irrelevance, that she worked 'for God' and that her prosecution was unfair since many other women surgeons had been left undisturbed. Perhaps they were less successful, for Peretta claimed that she had 'many sick persons or patients under her care who required essential remedies and visitation from her'. When her case was deferred until February she asked permission to visit them, but this was refused. In the meantime Peretta was ordered to remove 'the box or banner or sign which she had caused to be hung before her house after the manner of a public surgeon'. Her books 'on the said art of surgery' were also to be deposited at an official's office, to be examined by four physicians of Paris and other per-

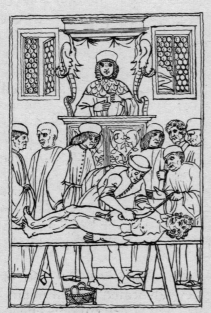

89   An anatomy lesson

sons. What happened to the intrepid Peretta we do not know. But, since she had been summoned previously and had gone on with her work, presumably she continued to defy the medical powers again on her release from the Châtelet where she had been imprisoned.

In 1436, the despised surgeons, who had been agitating for sometime to be accepted as scholars of the university, were granted the right to 'be reputed scholars and enjoy the privileges and liberties' conceded to the other sworn scholars of the university, provided that they attended the lectures of the masters of Paris teaching in the faculty of medicine. This was still regarded as the superior branch of the profession and the antagonism between surgery and medicine continued into the modern period. Nevertheless there were during the Middle Ages many educated physicians who were keenly interested in surgery and did a great deal to develop it. Here again it was Salerno which made the earliest contribution to the advance of the art. During the thirteenth century a book was written there—obviously a compilation—under the pseudonym of the Four Masters. This contains many advanced ideas for the conduct of surgical operations. Treatment for fracture of the skull, trepanning, is described in detail. Cold must especially be avoided when operating on a patients' head, it declares. The air of the operating room must be artificially warmed, hot plates should surround the head during the operation. A modern note is sounded by strict injunctions that absolute cleanliness is essential on the part of the surgeon, even to the avoidance of eating onions and leeks that might infect the air!

North Italian surgeons insisted on natural closure of wounds. To secure this they advocated a preliminary cleansing with wine which had an antiseptic effect. They then brought the edges of the wound together.

not allowing wine or anything else to remain inside so
that dry, adhesive surfaces could be obtained. Nature,
they said, would of itself produce a viscous fluid as the
means of union. Plastic surgery, which seems so
essentially a modern art, was practised before the end
of the Middle Ages by the Brancas, father and son.
Mutilated noses, lips and ears were successfully treated
by them, and in 1456 a description was written of the
grafting of skin by Antonio, the son, from the upper arm
of his patient to provide a new nose:

> And he inserted the remains of the mutilated nose
> into the skin of the upper arm, and bound them up so
> tightly the man could not even move his head. After
> 15–20 days, Branca little by little cut open the bit
> of flesh that adhered to the nose and reformed it into
> nostrils with such skill that the eye could scarcely
> detect where it had been joined on, and all facial
> deformity was completely removed. Branca healed
> many wounds which it seemed that no resource of
> medical art could cure.

France also had its brilliant surgeons, among the
most famous being Henri de Mondeville and Guy de
Chauliac. The former, a lecturer at Paris in the latter
half of the thirteenth century, was a pioneer in antiseptic surgery. One of his teachers, Jean Pitard,
surgeon of Philippe le Bel, was described as being 'most
skilful and expert in surgery'. It is to the fourteenth-
century Guy de Chauliac, however, that the title 'the
Father of Modern Surgery' has been given. He describes
the use of anaesthesia before an operation:

> Some surgeons prescribe medicaments such as
> opium, the juice of the morel, hyoscyamus, man-
> drake, ivy, hemlock, lettuce, which send the patient
> to sleep so that incision may not be felt. A new

sponge is soaked in the juice of the above and
dried in the sun; before use water is added to the
sponge then held under the patient's nose until he
goes to sleep.

Chauliac among other matters discusses operations for
hernia. He does not advise surgical treatment unless it is
to save the patient's life, but recommends the wearing
of a truss specially made and fitted, to suit the individual
needing it. A Flemish surgeon, Yperman, used the
oesophagus tube for artificial feeding about this time,
and dental care was studied by many physicians. A
special body of 'dentators' grew up to deal with teeth
and Chauliac enumerates the instruments they should
use—scrapers, rasps, spatumina, and many different
forms of probes, scalpels, tooth trephines and files. The
dental instrument for extraction—the pelican—was
also invented in France in the fourteenth century.

To take a last look at the practice of medicine and
surgery in the fifteenth century just before the dawn of
the Renaissance we must move back to Italy. A judge
had lost his young son through an unknown illness.
The family physician, Bernard Tornius, wrote to the
father proposing that, in order to try to prevent the
judge's other children from succumbing to the same
disease, an autopsy should be performed on the child's
body:

Worshipful Judge, I grieve over thy sad lot, for to
lose one's offspring is hard, harder to lose a son and
hardest to lose him by a disease not yet fully understood by doctors. But for the sake of the other
children, I think that to have seen his internal
organs will be of the greatest utility.

The report on the autopsy which follows is marked by
two qualities which are far more characteristic of

medieval thought and expression than is generally
recognised, namely, the clarity and directness with
which he states his facts, and the logic he uses to draw
deductions from his findings. Another unexpected
characteristic is the stress which Tornius lays on
preventive medicine and treatment in order, if possible,
to guard against a repetition of the same illness in the
judge's remaining children.

Another surgeon who flourished in the first half of the
fifteenth century, Leonard of Bertipaglia, wrote a
treatise on surgery for the benefit of his eleven year old
son, Fabricius: 'I swear by the living God and truly
Crucified to make no false statement to you, my son,
in this my book.' He then enumerates eight points which
the perfect surgeon ought to possess. Absolutely essential are

> light hands, expeditious in operating, lest you cause
> the patient pain. . . . For you heard him who said
> that I had light and expeditious hands when I
> extracted for him that bit of bone lodged in the
> hollow of the brain with that instrument of parch-
> ment through a small hole in the broken bone.

The operation was successful and Leonard proceeded to discuss the ventricles of the brain as being the
seat of particular activities: 'the first anterior ventricle
in which imagination takes place, the middle ventricle
in which cogitation or reasoning goes on, the third
posterior ventricle where retentive acts take place.'
From this it seems that the Middle Ages recognised
three, instead of the actual four ventricles. This view
persisted for centuries and localisation of function in the
brain was not seriously discussed until the mid-nin-
teenth century.

Along with obvious advances, however, medicine
and surgery still went hand in hand with magic and

astrology. Leonard himself solemnly quotes a cure for pest from Peter of Abano, who 'learned it from demons when he had exorcised them'. The archangel Sathael also taught men astrological medicine after his fall, Leonard assures us. Indeed, astrology was to remain on university syllabuses of medical faculties into modern times. As to reliance on tradition, as late as 1464 John of Arezzo—a well-known physician—dedicated his book on the heart to Piero de Medici, stating that the long list of medicine and drugs he recommends is drawn from the great physicians of the past, especially from the works of Avicenna the Arab.

> For in these matters I would not presume to add anything of my own. Since the richest treasures have been found rather by the opinion of the ancients than by reason, it is better for anyone to acquiesce, rather than to attempt something new.

Yet, despite this reluctance to abandon traditional teaching, superstitious practices and beliefs, despite the comparatively slow progress of medical research during the medieval period, great advances were undoubtedly made.

After the collapse of the Roman Empire and the almost complete destruction of classical learning in the West, the platform rebuilt so laboriously by medieval scholars, scientists, surgeons and physicians became the foundation on which it was possible for the no less astounding achievements of modern times to be erected.

10

SCIENTISTS AND TECHNOLOGISTS

Men try to discover the secret power in nature, which
profits them not at all, their sole desire being to gain
knowledge. With the same perverted aim they study
magic arts. . . . As for me I do not wish to know the
courses of the stars and all sacrilegious mysteries, I
hate.

THIS attitude of St Augustine, Bishop of Hippo in
North Africa, one of the early Church fathers whose
teaching had great influence throughout the Middle
Ages, is typical of the approach of the western Christian hierarchy to mere secular knowledge. Anything
that savoured of 'novelty' was anathema and the study
of the 'power in nature' unless it could be brought to
agree with the Church's teaching, was frowned upon.
Nevertheless the search for secular knowledge went on.
The pursuit of 'magic arts' and the study of the 'courses
of the stars' persisted until far into the modern period.
But the greatest impetus to the scientific impulse came
in the twelfth and thirteenth centuries, mainly through
the introduction into western Christendom of the
scientific works of Greek writers, especially those of
Aristotle. These entered the West chiefly as translations
into Latin from Arabic versions.

This advancement in secular knowledge was accompanied by a more critical attitude among certain
scholars towards the conservatism of ecclesiastical

authority. Adelard of Bath was one of these who, early in the twelfth century was stimulated by the Arabic works he was translating into Latin. This led him to challenge the ancient authority of the Church and the medieval subservience to tradition. In his book *Natural Questions* Adelard writes:

> I learned from my Arabian masters under the leading of reason; you, however, captivated by the appearance of authority, follow your halter. For what else should authority be called but a halter? Just as brute beasts are led where one wills by a halter, so authority of past writers leads not a few of you into danger, held and bound as you are by bestial credulity.

But conservative churchmen did not accept the new teachings. Stephen, Bishop of Tournai, is one of those who headed the fight against 'modernism'. In a letter to the Pope about 1202 he bitterly complains:

> The studies of sacred letters among us are fallen into the workshop of confusion, while both disciples applaud novelties alone and masters watch out for glory rather than learning. Faculties called liberal having lost their pristine liberty are sunk in such servitude that adolescents with long hair impudently usurp their professorships and beardless youths sit in the seat of their seniors, and those who don't yet know how to be disciples strive to be named masters. These write *summulae* [commentaries on great works] moistened with drool and dribble, but unseasoned with the salt of philosophers.

The bishop's accusations have an almost modern ring. The new attitude he complains about was the result mainly of the translation of Aristotle's *Physics* and *Metaphysics*, early in the thirteenth century. Up till then only his *Logic* had been known to scholars. Many conservatives like Stephen realised the dangers of the new learning to orthodox theology. Almost as if in panic, attempts were made to try to stem the newly freed and swiftly flowing stream of Greek scientific ideas. In 1210 a decree was published declaring that in the University of Paris 'neither the books of Aristotle on natural philosophy, nor their commentaries are to be read in Paris in public or in secret, and this we forbid on pain of excommunication'.

The fight between science and orthodox religion had begun. The University of Toulouse, in the more free-thinking south, came down on the side of modernism, advertising that 'Aristotle's books, forbidden in Paris, could be read there by all those who cared to penetrate into the secrets of nature'. By 1231 the Church was forced to compromise and in April that year the Pope declared:

> since, as we have learned, the books on nature which were prohibited at Paris are said to contain both useful and useless matter we command that you examine the same books . . . and entirely exclude what you find there to be erroneous or harmful so that the rest may be studied without delay.

In response to this need St Thomas Aquinas (*d.* 1274) retranslated Aristotle's works and in his famous book, the *Summa*, drew up a commentary and attempted to reconcile Aristotle's pagan and scientific ideas with the Church's doctrine.

Arabic translations also helped to introduce the pseudo-science of alchemy into western Christendom. It was based on Aristotle's theory of the 'Four Elements'. In this, matter was held to be composed of earth, water, fire and air. It was also held that all material bodies had four properties—the hot and the

moist, and their con-
traries, the cold and the
dry. By experiment it
had been found that
cold, wet water could,
when heated, be chan-
ged into hot, wet air. In
the same way, it was be-
lieved that bodies could
be transmuted into the
primordial matter of
which they were all com-
posed, if only the agent

90   The alchemist Thomas Norton
at work

capable of promoting this change could be discovered.
The search for this agent, known as the 'Philosopher's
Stone,' was the main object of alchemy, for by its means
it was believed also that base metals could be transmuted into silver or gold. In addition, through its
agency, the elixir of life could be made which would
confer immortality on any who drank it.

For the uneducated and superstitious to enter a
medieval alchemist's laboratory was a terrifying
experience. The experimenters were regarded as
magicians, in league with the devil. We have a picture
of a fifteenth-century alchemist at work, the moon
shining through a Gothic window behind, his face lit
up by the glare from his athanor, or furnace by means
of which the 'Great Work' is proceeding; above the
flames an egg-shaped container, hermetically sealed, is
being heated. All round are other furnaces, for many
are needed for the preliminary stages of the work; on
nearby benches fire-clay crucibles, metal mortars, glass
flasks and retorts are scattered, as well as furnace rakes,
tongs for handling red-hot containers and funnels and
strainers.

The lore of the alchemist was carefully guarded and

91   Furnace and stills designed by
Leonardo da Vinci

his writing was clothed in cryptic phrases and symbolic terms. Colours too had their hidden meaning when used in alchemical illustrations: a red king represented sophic sulphur, a white queen sophic mercury, and these substances were not the same as ordinary sulphur or mercury. The royal personages could also represent gold and silver. The colours of the Great Work were often expressed as birds—the crow, black; the swan, white; the phoenix, red.

Nicolas Flammel (1330–1418), who worked with his devoted wife Perrenelle, was one of the most famous of the medieval goldmakers. He claimed to have found the secret of the Great Work written in a mysterious 'gilded book, very old and large, with a cover of brass, well bound, all engraven with letters of strange figures'. Flammel also decorated the arcade of the churchyard of the Innocents in Paris with alchemical designs in symbolic colours.

A fifteenth-century monk, whose pseudonym was Basil Valentine, has also left a treatise known as *The Twelve Keys*, in which twelve designs portray alchemical symbolism. These, Valentine claimed, show how the doors to the 'most ancient Stone of our Ancestors and the most secret Fountain of All Health' are to be found. The first key shows a king and queen who represent the sun and moon, or the gold and silver of popular alchemy, the sophic sulphur and mercury in the secret lore. The fierce grey wolf symbolises antimony—a metal thought to have powerful properties, especially that of purification. The wolf's body is to be burned to ashes in a great fire to liberate the king. This process of purifying the gold with antimony is done three times and is indicated in the picture by the three flowers held by the queen. The wooden-legged man with a scythe is Saturn, symbol of the dull metal lead which is to be transmuted into silver or gold. The fan of peacocks' feathers with its varied colours represents the humours of the body.

The aims of alchemists varied greatly. Some were mystics and idealists who sought to change their own natures through their experiments and the symbolic philosophy which accompanied them. The modern psycho-analyst, Carl Jung, has worked out the philosophy and some of the underlying meaning of alchemy. The philosophic alchemists thought that, if they could prove that in the material world base metals could be transmuted into gold, in a similar way base qualities within man could be transmuted into those of the noblest kind. For one of the fundamental beliefs of the Middle Ages, derived from Plato, was that man and the universe correspond in nature and structure: 'as above, so below'—in other words the macrocosm or universe is repeated in the microcosm or smaller universe of each individual.

In contrast to the idealists were the charlatans who obtained an initial supply of gold from their patrons, deluding them by promising that by its help they could turn a large supply of lead into gold. For the precious metals, like everything else in nature, it was believed, only multiplied in their own species. The initial gift of gold would become the seed or Philosopher's Stone through which more gold would be produced. Thomas Norton of Bristol in the fifteenth century, himself a most efficient alchemist, was no charlatan. In poetic fashion he pointed out that 'true men' involved no one in any cost but bore the brunt of the Great Work themselves:

> *The true men search and seek all alone*
> *In hope to find the delectable stone,*
> *And for that they would that no man should have loss,*
> *They prove and seek all at their own cost.*
> *So their own purses they will not spare*
> *They make their coffers thereby full bare.*

The picture of a weeping wife begging for money to buy bread for herself and her child, while her husband fanatically pursues his search for the secret that will make them all wealthy beyond dreams, tells the same tale.

There were also the 'puffers', so called from their constant use of the bellows by which they kept up the heat of their furnaces. These sincerely believed that persistence would bring success. The pseudo-Geber was one of these. His *Sum of Perfection*, written in the early fourteenth century, was the main chemical text-book of medieval Christendom. It was men like him who paved the way for the later science of chemistry.

The courses of the stars, so indifferently regarded by

92 Nicole Oresme presents his work to Charles V of France

Augustine, were studied throughout the Middle Ages with the greatest interest, since (it was thought) they directly influenced both human destinies and historical events. Aristotle had taught that the fixed stars had a regular, circular motion, whereas the movements of the planets were irregular. The fixed stars were held, therefore, to control the ordered course of nature, the succession of seasons, of day and night, whereas the planets influenced the course of history, day-to-day events, including birth and death.

It was also believed that by divination the future could be foretold. According to the day of the week on which a new year began the general characteristics of the following twelve months could be learned:

> If the Kalends of January shall be on the Lord's Day, the winter will be good and mild and warm; the spring, windy and the summer dry. Good vintage, increasing flocks, and honey will be abundant; the old men will die and peace will be made.

When a child was born, an astrologer was often employed to cast the infant's horoscope. According to the position of the planets and stars at the moment of birth, so it was believed the child would be famous or unknown, wise or unlettered, long- or short-lived, rich or poor, and live a life of ease or one of danger. The most suitable profession or trade for the child could also be forecast. If born under Mars he should choose to become a smith or a soldier, if under the sign of Venus then an artistic profession, or perhaps that of a courtier should be chosen.

Gerbert, later Pope Sylvester II, was supposed to have studied astrology and other arts in Spain under the Saracens. There, it was said, he also 'learned what the song and flight of birds portend, and to summon ghostly figures from the lower world'. For the astro-

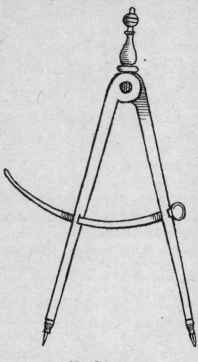

93 Compasses

loger, like the alchemist, was suspected of being a magician and Gerbert was described as 'the best necromancer in France, whom demons obeyed in all that he required of them, day and night, because of the great sacrifices which he offered and his prayers and fastings and magic books and great diversity of rings and candles'. Even his acquisition of the papacy was ascribed to the aid of a demon and it was said that he was enabled to solve arithmetical problems by the help of a spirit which he had enclosed within a golden head. To be associated at all with Arabic learning was to run the risk of being regarded as the familiar of demons and spirits, if not actually in the tutelage of the Prince of Darkness himself.

By the end of the fourteenth century, however, scholars increasingly began to attack the practice of astrology. Critical writings of the period show that a more scientific attitude was emerging in many branches of learning. Nicole Oresme (*92*), one of the greatest mathematicians of the fourteenth century, who died in 1382 as Bishop of Lisieux, wrote strongly against occult practices. Although gross superstition and a belief in magic persisted in the court of his patron Charles V of

France, Oresme tried to point out the differences between astronomy proper and the pseudo-science of astrology.

Jean de Dons of Padua was another scholar with a more rationalistic approach who was trying to discourage astrological practices: 'not through any great devotion to the Church, or because the said practices are forbidden, but because he recognises clearly the error of those who waste their time on such forecasts and deceive great lords.' Jean, we are told,

> lived with the Count of Vertus from whom, by reason of his triple science—philosophy, medicine and astronomy—he received in wages 2,000 florins, or thereabouts, per annum. This Master Jean has in his time made great and important astrological machines for great clerks of Italy, Germany and Hungary. Among other instruments he has made is one called by some the sphere or clock of heavenly motions. In this machine, by means of multiplication of countless wheels, the movements of the planetary signs, with their circles and epicycles and differences are shown; and for each planet in the aforesaid sphere, is shown its particular movement, so that at any moment day or night can be seen in what sign or degree both planets and fixed stars in the heavens are situated. Moreover, this sphere is so constructed that notwithstanding the multitude of wheels . . . the whole movement is governed by a single counterpoise. Consequently, all learned in astronomy, philosophy and medicine declare that no record exists of the making of so subtle or precise an instrument as this machine.

Nicole Oresme, Jean's contemporary, refers to such an artificial sphere as an aid to the understanding of the movement of the world and the heavens. Oresme goes

on to outline the arrangement of the universe as defined
in the fourteenth century:

> The earth is round like a ball and philosophers say
> that the sphere of the world is made up of the heavens
> and the four elements. First comes the earth, massive
> and round, although not perfectly round, for there
> are mountains and valleys. But if the earth were
> viewed from the moon, it would appear to be round,
> and the eclipse of the moon, the result of the earth's
> shadow, shows the earth to be round. The earth is
> at the centre of the Universe because it is the heaviest
> of the four elements.

Although the medieval scientists were right in believing
the earth to be round, they were wrong in asserting its
position to be at the centre of the universe. It was assumed also that the earth was fixed and immovable because Biblical writers had declared that 'the world is stabilised and cannot be moved'. Nicholas of Cusa in the fifteenth century questioned this concept, but not until 1543 did Copernicus show that the sun was the centre round which earth and planets revolved.

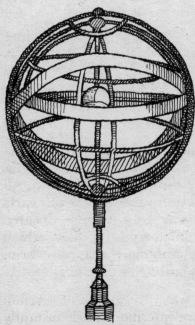

94   Nicole Oresme's armillary
sphere

In Oresme's cosmography, however, the earth was surrounded by an incomplete watery sphere, both of which in turn were enclosed by a sphere of air. Round this is the sphere of fire. Above these four elements of earth, water, air and fire is the sky. This is divided into the successive spheres of the moon, of Mercury, Venus, the Sun, Mars, Jupiter and Saturn, with the sphere of the fixed stars beyond; other spheres there are, Oresme tells us, but speculations about these do not belong to natural philosophy or astronomy.

In the realm of botany, medieval knowledge depended largely, as with the other branches of science, on ancient books and authorities. *The Herbal* of Dioscorides, a first-century writer, was used mainly by those who wanted to learn about the medicinal properties of plants. *The Herbal* was widely used until the seventeenth century. A Spanish physician at the end of the Middle Ages wrote:

Dioscorides did seek out those herbs, trees, plants, beasts and minerals of the which he made those six books which are so celebrated in all the world whereby he gat great fame and glory . . . and there hath remained more fame of him by writing them, than although he had gotten many cities with his warlike acts.

Another famous herbal was that ascribed to Apuleius Barbarus. It was compiled around the year A.D. 5. All the medieval herbals which were based on the early ones are full of magical lore. A frequently repeated account of the uprooting of the mandrake plant, which was regarded as closely resembling the human form, is originally given by Apuleius:

It shineth at night, altogether like a lamp. When first thou seest its head, there inscribe thou it instantly with iron, lest it fly from thee; its virtue is so mickle and so famous that it will fly immediately from an unclean man. . . . When thou seest its hands and feet, then tie thou it up. Then tie the other end of the rope to a hungry dog's neck. Cast meat next before him, but out of reach do so that the dog in trying to seize the meat, do jerk the plant up with him. Then take the plant, twist it and wring the ooze out of its leaves into a glass ampulla.

The plant was noted for its soporific qualities and was used as an anaesthetic before operations and during child-birth.

Several thirteenth-century authors of herbals did more than make mere slavish copies of earlier works. Albertus Magnus (1206–80), a voluminous writer on scientific, theological and philosophical subjects, wrote a book on plant life based on one by Damascenus written before the birth of Christ. Albertus makes several original observations, among them the fact that vines sometimes produced tendrils. He follows this by the correct conclusion that the tendrils were a potential bunch of grapes which had failed to develop. Albertus also attempted to classify flowers into types. He has only three, however: the bird form (like violets and dead-nettles), the pyramid or bell form (convolvulus), and the star form (the rose).

95   The Dominican Albertus Magnus

A contemporary of Albertus wrote a herbal which contained even more original observation. This was by

Rufinus of Genoa. He states in his preface that he intends to rely on early authorities for much of his information, then adds, 'After that, I'll speak'. Among other detailed descriptions he gives one of the long *aristologia* (Birthwort or Pipe Vine):

> It has long pointed leaves and a yellow flower and a long root. The round *aristologia* has round leaves and a black flower and a round apple on its root. The fruit of both are called by the common people terrumalium—they hang from the branches. Or they are called *mellumcelli* by the same laymen.

Again, Rufinus describes camphor as a gum which will burn on water as bitumen does in oil, if it is placed on something light in the water while it is burning. 'This I have proved,' he adds, 'and it is true.' Here again is observation and experiment, not a mere repetition of traditional lore.

Simon Cordo of Genoa also wrote a herbal about 1292, based on knowledge gained during wide travels. He searched for plants on mountains and in valleys, by streams and on the plain. In Crete he talked to an old crone and from her gained the names and properties of herbs and plants. A male Greek who knew Latin also helped Simon. Indeed Cordo, Rufinus and Albertus Magnus obviously devoted much time to botanical research and were among the first medieval scholars to lay the foundations of botanical study as a science.

Herbals were illustrated, and no doubt aimed to show plants in their natural shapes and colours, but, since many of their compilers merely copied from an earlier manuscript, the appearance of the plant became farther and farther removed from its actual likeness. In addition, plants were often shown intertwined with the insect or animal whose bites or poison it was supposed to counteract. For instance, the plantain is often represented with a serpent or scorpion, and the mandrake plant is portrayed with a human form, sometimes male, sometimes female. A book of medicines from animals was often included with a herbal. These give a stylised representation of an animal with directions regarding the cure to be obtained from it. This comprised not only medicines or lotions made from various organs but also those made from animal excrement.

The study of animals was pursued most scientifically at the Sicilian court of Frederick II (1212–50). This young man was also Emperor of Germany but had been brought up in Sicily, which he much preferred to his northern realms. Sicily, brought successively under the sway of Moslems, Normans and Germans, was the meeting-place of Arabic, Greek and northern cultures. Frederick, intensely interested in animals and birds— especially in falcons—collected a menagerie which travelled everywhere with him, even over the Alps to Germany. The Sultan of Egypt sent him a present of a giraffe—the first to be seen in medieval Europe. It caused great excitement where it went. Leopards, panthers, hawks and falcons were all used by the emperor for hunting. Frederick wrote and illustrated with his own hand a book *About the Art of Hunting and Falconry*. His bird sketches are extraordinarily true to life; brilliantly coloured and exact to the smallest detail, they are obviously the result of the keenest observation. The same originality is seen in the text. If Frederick quotes Aristotle, it is usually to disagree with him. When he gives information not his own, it has usually been gained from some distant expert, summoned by the emperor to his court. Frederick was not content to make statements without proving them by experiment. He brought experts from Egypt to Apulia to test out the possibility of hatching eggs by the heat of the sun. Because of this refusal to accept statements without practical proof, as well as the recording of facts after close personal observation, Frederick's book has rightly been regarded as the forerunner of later treatises in scientific zoology.

The emperor also attracted many scholars to his court. Among them was Michael Scot who made a summary for the emperor of the Arabian Avicenna's *Concerning Animals*. Michael also wrote on astrology, physiognomy and meteorology, while Leonard of Pisa, a mathematician of genius, wrote a treatise on the abacus for Frederick.

King Roger of Sicily, Frederick's grandfather, had also been interested in scientific subjects but it was geography which he pursued most ardently. Not content with the work of Arabic writers the king summoned famous travellers to his court to give an account of their adventures. Only those facts which tallied with the evidence of others satisfied Roger, and these he had recorded by an Arabian scholar Edrisi in 1154. The results of their explorations were engraved on a silver map. Moslems had first penetrated into the lands in Africa south of the Sahara during the tenth century, but it was not until the twelfth that Christians learned of a civilisation in the interior of the continent.

Ramon Lull (*d.* 1315/16), the Majorcan missionary to the Moslems, wrote the earliest eye-witness account of the journey of a Christian across the Sahara. This man, the messenger of a cardinal,

found a caravan of 6,000 camels laden with salt leaving a town named Tibalbert and journeying to that country where the source of the River Damiata [the Nile] is. So many people lived there that all the salt was sold within 15 days. These men were black and worshipped idols. In the land is an island in a great

lake where lives a dragon to whom all make sacrifices
. . . and the people were astonished at the messenger,
for he was white and a Christian, for never had they
heard of a Christian in that land before.

Exploration into the interior of Africa continued
after this, though intermittently, but even in the six-
teenth century African natives were described as
'men with faces, teeth and tails like dogs'.

One of the earliest voyages by a Christian along the
western seaboard of Africa of which any record remains
was that undertaken by a Spanish Franciscan friar
about 1350. His companions were Moors and they
reached the coast of Sierra Leone and mention the
island of Shubro. The Este world map of about 1450
appears to have been drawn from information left by

96   The Polos at the court of Kublai Khan

this friar. Other medieval maps witness to the exploration and recordings of other journeys and voyages into the interior and along the coast of the continent.

The penetration of Asia by Europeans in the thirteenth century was largely brought about by a growing desire to convert the Asiatics and gain them as allies in the struggle against the Moslems. Stories also circulated about this time of a mythical Christian king, Prester John, who ruled in the East, and missionaries were sent out to search for him. One of the earliest of these was the Franciscan, John of Plano Carcopini, who arrived at Karakorum in Outer Mongolia in 1245. The trail blazed by missionaries was soon followed by traders, although Marco Polo of Venice, who left a wonderful description of his travels and of China, was a diplomat rather than a missionary or trader. He tells us of the density of population in China, of its vast fields of rice and millet, of its enormous towns '100 miles in circuit, with ten principal markets attended three days a week by 40–50,000 people'. Although the fall of the Mongol dynasty later closed China to foreigners, nevertheless traders were stimulated to find alternative routes to the Indies. In fact, the journeys into Africa and Asia and the voyages along the coast to Sierra Leone had far-reaching effects. Where, before, their world had centres round the Mediterranean, its eastern boundaries those of the eastern empire, now the world had expanded, and seemed suddenly limitless. Such an attitude spurred on men like Prince Henry the Navigator, Columbus and Magellan to promote or undertake later voyages. But the initial impulse to go out and explore had come originally from the intrepid sailors and travellers of the thirteenth and fourteenth centuries.

Besides the efforts of scholars, sailors and explorers, the change in the everyday life and intellectual outlook

97   An early post-mill

can be attributed to technical advances. It is not known who first thought of using water power for driving hammers, bellows and stamping-mills or for grinding corn and pulping material for paper. After the tenth century the number of water-mills increased steadily.

In Aube, in France, while there were only 14 in the eleventh century, there were nearly 200 in the thirteenth. In central Europe water-mills seem to have been established as early as the eighth century. Their use spread later to Germany and Scandinavia, while Italians built the first German paper-mill near Nuremberg in 1389.

Windmills were also used extensively in flat areas. In the Low Countries one was erected about 1430 to aid in draining the marshes—although it was not until the seventeenth century that they were generally used for that purpose. The earliest mention of a windmill in western Europe is of one in Normandy about 1180. The use of water power was a great boon during the shortage of labour that followed the Black Death. It also enabled more work to be done and more goods to be produced in less time. This helped Europe build up her commercial prosperity during the twelfth and thirteenth centuries.

But, of all the technical changes in Europe, making paper on a large scale perhaps had the most far-reaching effect. From Roman imperial times, parchment had been used for permanent records. This was specially prepared from animal skins which had been shaved and thinned, then dried on a stretching frame. Calf skin provided the finest parchment, which, after treatment, was called vellum. Parchment, however, was expensive and this, together with the fact that all medieval books were handwritten, made them costly to produce. Paper-making—originally a Chinese invention—was introduced into Spain, at Jativa, by Jews or Arabs about 1150. Briefly, the manufacture of paper followed six main processes. The raw material— linen, cotton, straw or wood—was reduced to pulp in water. At first a hand-worked stamping-mill with wooden pestles was used. Between 1269 and 1276 water power was employed at Fabriano, in Italy, to lift metal pistons up and down to pulp the wet material which was now more efficiently broken down by the improved machinery.

At the right moment, the pulp was put into a vat in charge of a vatman. He held a mould, a sort of tray with a wire mesh and base, edged with a movable 'deckle', which formed the sides of the tray and regulated the size and edges of the paper. The mould was plunged into the pulp and brought out face upwards. The surplus liquid drained off through the mesh. After shaking the mould from side to side to settle the remaining pulp evenly on the mesh, the vatman removed the wooden deckle and handed the mould to a 'coucher'. This man carried the paper on the mould to a pile of felting. Here he waited until the paper was sufficiently set, then deftly turned it out from the mould on to the top layer of felt which had been cut to the required size. A fresh piece of felt was put over it, and the same process was repeated until a pile of 144 sheets of paper had been couched, each lying between its sheet of felt. A worker called the layman then carried the pile of damp paper and felts to be pressed. Afterwards the paper was dried, usually by hanging it on

98   Stages in making a parchment book

fine ropes of hair. The final process was to dip each
sheet in a solution of gelatine rendered from hoofs,
horns and hides of animals. After being dried again,
the surface—hard and impervious—was well adapted
to writing with a quill pen.

It was later found, however, that this surface was
quite unsuitable for printing in the Chinese manner
with wooden blocks, a process which had been followed
in China since the eighth century. European printers
set themselves to overcome this difficulty and found
that, by using metal types and a hand-press, they could
print on both sides of the paper. This epoch-making
invention was in part due to John Gutenberg of Mainz,
but presses were soon set up in other European countries. By the close of the fifteenth century over nine
million books had been printed from metal type. These
discoveries of paper-making and printing brought
about a revolution as great as, if not greater, than
Columbus' discovery of America. Through the medium
of printed books the ideas of Antiquity were dissemina-
ted throughout Christendom. This classical learning
had largely brought about the splendid flowering
of twelfth-century civilisation. It was also to be the
chief impetus of the sixteenth-century renaissance.
Both developments blossomed from the same plant—
from roots far down in medieval soil. This living

product of classical learning though sometimes cut back, was nurtured through the centuries and was destined to blossom again, enriched and renewed, in the period which has come to be known as the Modern Age.

CHRONOLOGY

Rulers and Popes	Religious and Monastic	Military and Political
	354 St Augustine of Hippo born	
	379 Death of St Basil of Pontus	
	412 St Cassius at Marseilles	**410** Alaric takes Rome
	430 Death of St Augustine	**476 Fall of Rome**
	480–543 St Benedict of Nursia	
489 Theodoric the Goth King of Italy		
511 Death of Clovis the Frank		
526 Death of Theodoric		
		550 Avars invade Europe
		560 Lombards invade Italy
	575 Death of Cassiodorus	
590–604 Gregory the Great, Pope	**581** Monte Cassino destroyed	
	594 Death of Gregory, Bishop of Tours	
	609 St Columban founds Luxeuil	
	622 Hegira of Mohammed	
		635 Moslems conquer Syria, Persia, Egypt and Libya
639 Death of Dagobert Merovingian King of the Franks		
	692 Willibrord converts Frisians	
		711–6 Moslems conquer Spain and Portugal
	721 Moslems sack Luxeuil	
		732 Charles Martel defeats Moslems at Poitiers
741 Death of Charles Martel		

Artistic and Literary	Scientific, Geographical and Commercial	British Events
c. **350** Donatus writes his grammar		
		410 Romans gradually abandon Britain
413–26 St Augustine writes *The City of God*		
		449–57 Foundation of English Settlements in Britain
523–4 Boethius writes *The Consolations of Philosophy*		
c. **525** Priscian writes his grammar		
	526 Death of Anthimus, Theodoric's Greek doctor	
		563 St Columba lands on Iona
		597 St Augustine in Kent
		616–32 Edwin of Northumbria
		633–55 Penda of Mercia
		633–41 Oswald of Northumbria, Deira and Bernicia
		731 The Venerable Bede writes his *Ecclesiastical History*

Rulers and Popes	Religious and Monastic	Military and Political
	754 St Boniface killed by Frisians	
768 Death of Pippin, King of Franks Charlemagne succeeds as king		
		793–5 Norse attack Lindisfarne and Ireland
		800 Charlemagne Emperor
814 Death of Charlemagne	**817** Benedict of Aniane impose Benedictine Rule in Frankish monasteries	
840 Death of Louis the Pious		
		855–62 Norse settle on Loire and Seine
		870 Treaty of Mersen
		878 Moslems conquer Sicily
	910 Abbey of Cluny founded	
		911 Norsemen settle in N. France
		925 Magyars attack Europe
936 Hugh, King of the Lombards		
973–83 Otto II, King of Germany		
983–1002 Otto III Emperor of Germany		
		987–1040 Fulk of Anjou
999–1003 Gerbert Pope Sylvester II		

Artistic and Literary	Scientific, Geographical and Commercial	British Events
		757–96 Offa of Mercia
782–96 Alcuin head of the Palace School		
c. **790** Angilbert begins the Church of Centula		
Late 8th-century, Odo of Metz builds Charlemagne's chapel at Aachen		
		802–39 Egbert of Wessex
During the 9th century Romanesque architecture develops	**850** Rhazes, famous Persian doctor born	
		871–99 Alfred the Great
		899–924 Edward the Elder
		925–40 Athelstan
		940–46 Edmund the Magnificent
		946–55 Edred—Dunstan his chief minister
		959–75 Edgar, King of all England
	980–1037 Avicenna Moorish doctor	
		991 Danish Conquest begins
		1013 Submission of England to Sweyne

Rulers and Popes	Religious and Monastic	Military and Political
		1020–53 Normans conquer South Italy
	1026 Abbot of St Vanne's pilgrimage to Jerusalem	
	1028 Death of Bishop Fulbert of Chartres	
		1071 Turkish victory at Manzikert
1073–Pope Hildebrand		**1077** Emperor Henry II submits at Canossa to Pope Gregory VII
	1079–1142 Peter Abelard	
1081–1118 Emperor Alexius (Comnenus)		
	1086 St Bruno founds Carthusian Order	
1088–99 Pope Urban II		
		1095–9 First Crusade
1108–37 Louis VI of France		
	1109 Death of St Anselm	
	1115–80 John of Salisbury	
	1117 Stephen Harding's *Charter of Love*	
	1122–51 Suger, Abbot of St Denis	
		1143 Arnold of Brescia's revolt in Italy
	1153 Death of St Bernard of Clairvaux	
1154 Death of Roger II of Sicily		
	1175 The Waldensians	

Artistic and Literary	Scientific, Geographical and Commercial	British Events
8th–11th centuries *The Song of Roland* developed		1017–35 Canute, King of England
		1033 Death of Queen Margaret of Scotland
		1066 Normans conquer England
		1066–87 William I
		1087–1100 William Rufus
		1100–35 Henry I
Early 12th-century Adelard of Bath writes *Natural Questions* embodying his scientific studies		
Gothic architecture develops		
c. 1120 The Alexiad		
		1135–54 Stephen
c. 1140 Gratian's *Decretum* written		
1141 Oderic Vitalis finishes *Ecclesiastical History*		
	1150 Paper made in Spain	
		1154–89 Henry II
		1170 Murder of Thomas Becket

Rulers and Popes	Religious and Monastic	Military and Political
		1204 Fourth Crusade. Constantinople captured
1208 Pope Innocent III *v.* Albigenses		
1212–50 Emperor Frederick II	**1214** Dominican Order of Friars founded	
	1223 Franciscan Order of Friars founded	
1226–70 Louis IX (Saint Louis)		
	1274 Death of St Bonaventure	
	1274 Death of St Thomas Aquinas	
	1280 Death of Albertus Magnus. These two worked to reconcile Aristotle's ideas with Catholic theology	
1285–1314 Philip IV of France (le Bel)		
	1312 The Knights Templars suppressed	
1317 Pope John XXII		
		1323 – 8 Social revolt in Flanders

Artistic and Literary	Scientific, Geographical and Commercial	British Events
	1180 First recorded windmill in Europe John of Salisbury writes his *Metalogicon*	
		1189–99 Richard I
		1199–1216 John
	1206–80 Albertus Magnus	
13th century Guillaume de Lorris writes *The Romance of the Rose* Marie de France writes her *lais*		
		1215 Issue of Magna Carta
		1216–72 Henry III
	1245 John of Plano Carcopino reaches Karakorum	
c. **1250** Villars de Honnecourt		
	1252 Gold coins minted in Italy	
1265 Dante born		
	1271–92 Marco Polo in China	**1272–1307** Edward I
1304–74 Petrarch		**1307–27** Edward II
		1327–77 Edward III
	1330–1418 Nicholas Flammel alchemist	
1338 Froissart born		
1344–50 Boccaccio writes *The Decameron*		*c.* **1340–1400** Chaucer
		1346–1453 The Hundred Years War

Artistic and Literary	Scientific, Geographical and Commercial	British Events
1364–80 Charles V of France		
1380–1422 Charles VI of France (married to Queen Isabella)		
1422–61 Charles VII (Minister Jacques Coeur)		
	1444 Death of St Bernadino of Italy	
		1453 Turks capture Constantinople
	1465–1536 Erasmus	
1483–98 Charles VIII of France		

Artistic and Literary	Scientific, Geographical and Commercial	British Events
	1348–50 Black Death in Europe Guy de Chauliac, surgeon	
		1377–99 Richard II
		1379 Henry Yevele, Richard II's master mason, designed the nave of Canterbury Cathedral
Jean de Meun completes *The Romance of the Rose*	**1382** Death of mathematician Nicole Oresme	
1402 Christine de Pisan		**1399–1413** Henry IV **1413–22** Henry V
	1415–61 Henry the Navigator John of Mainz develops art of typography	**1422–61** Henry VI
		1461–83 Edward IV
	1465 Printing from metal types reaches Italy	**1483** Edward V **1483–5** Richard III

SELECT BIBLIOGRAPHY

General

Christopher Brooke, *Europe in the Central Middle Ages*, Longmans, 1964

Cambridge Medieval History (Vols. 1–8), Cambridge, 1911–36

Joan Evans (Ed.), *The Flowering of the Middle Ages*, Thames and Hudson, 1966

H. A. L. Fisher, *A History of Europe* (Vol. I), Fontana Library, 1964

J. H. Robinson, *Medieval and Modern Times*, Ginn, 1944

R. W. Southern, *The Making of the Middle Ages*, Hutchinson, 1965

1 Charlemagne and Society

D. Bullough, *The Age of Charlemagne*, Elek, 1965

E. S. Duckett, *Alcuin, Friend of Charlemagne*, Macmillan, New York, 1951

A. J. Grant (Ed.), *Early Lives of Charlemagne*, King's Classics series, 1905

L. Halpen, *Études Critiques sur l'Histoire de Charlemagne*, Alcan, Paris, 1921

J. I. Mombert, *Charles the Great*, Kegan Paul, 1888

C. K. Scott-Moncrieff, *The Song of Roland*, Chapman and Hall, 1919

J. M. Wallace Hadrill, *The Barbarian West*, Hutchinson, 1164

L. Wallach, *Alcuin and Charlemagne*, Cornell 1959

2 Lords and Vassals

Marc Bloch, *Feudal Society* (2 Vols.), Routledge and Kegan Paul, 1962

—— *French Rural History*, Routledge and Kegan Paul, 1966

P. Boissonade, (tr. E. Power), *Life and Work in Medieval Europe*, Kegan Paul, 1927

Cambridge Economic History of Europe (Vol. I), Cambridge University Press

Joan Evans, *Medieval France* (Chapter II), Phaidon Press, 1957
F. L. Ganshof, *Feudalism*, Longmans, 1952
Iris Origo, *The Merchant of Prato* ('The Farm'), Cape, 1957
H. Pirenne, *Economic and Social History of Medieval Europe*, Kegan
   Paul, 1936

3 Townsmen and Traders

R. Latouche, *The Birth of Western Economy*, Methuen, 1961
A. R. Lewis, *Naval Power and Trade in the Mediterranean* 500–1100,
   Princeton, 1951
—— *The Northern Seas*, Princeton, 1958
W. Map (tr. M. R. James), *De Nugis Curialum* (see story of Scaeva
   and Ollo), Cymmrodorion Society, 1923
Iris Origo, *The Merchant of Prato*, Cape, 1957
E. Power, *Medieval People*, Pelican, 1939

4 Women and Wives

T. Austin, *Two Fifteenth Century Cookery Books*, Early English Text
   Society, 1888
H. S. Bennett, *The Pastons and their England*, Cambridge, 1932
C. G. Crump and E. F. Jacobs (Ed.), *The Legacy of the Middle Ages*,
   Oxford, 1926
F. J. Furnivall, *Book of Precedence*, Early English Text Society, 1869
E. Power, *The Goodman of Paris*, Blackwell, 1928
T. Wright, *Womankind in Western Europe*, Groombridge, 1869
—— *The Knight of La Tour-Landry*, Early English Text Society,
   1868

5 Pilgrims and Crusaders

Sir E. Barker, *The Crusades*, Oxford, 1932
M. Chibnall (tr.), *Historia Pontificalis of John of Salisbury*, Nelson,
   1956
E. A. S. Dawes (tr.), *The Alexiad*, Kegan Paul, 1928
R. M. T. Hill (tr.), *Gesta Francorum*, Nelson, 1962
Joinville and Villehardouin (M. R. B. Shaw, tr.), *Chronicles of the
   Crusader*, Penguin, 1963
J. J. Jusserand, *English Wayfaring Life in the Middle Ages*, Benn,
   1950

A. C. Krey, *The First Crusade:* the accounts of eye-witnesses and participants, Princeton, 1921

M. Letts (Ed.), *The Travels of Pero Tafur,* Routledge, 1929

R. A. Newall, *The Crusades,* Bell, 1930

G. R. Potter (tr.), *The Autobiography of Ousama,* Broadway Medieval Library, 1929

Sir S. Runciman, *History of the Crusades* (3 Vols.), Cambridge, 1951–4

Aubrey Stewart (tr.), *Wanderings of Brother Felix Fabri,* Palestine Pilgrims' Trust Society, 1893

G. F. Warner (Ed.), *Miracles of Nostre Dame,* Roxburghe Club, 1885

William Wey, *Itineraries,* Roxburghe Club, 1857

6 Monks and Friars

J. J. Bagley and P. B. Rowley, *A Documentary History of England,* Pelican, 1966

L. Bieler, *Ireland, Harbinger of the Middle Ages,* Oxford, 1963

G. G. Coulton, *From St Francis to Dante,* London, 1906

—— *Five Centuries of Religion* (I), Cambridge, 1929

J. Decarreaux (C. Haldane, tr.), *Monks and Civilisation,* Allen and Unwin, 1964

J. Evans, *Monastic Life at Cluny,* Oxford, 1930

D. Knowles, *Saints and Scholars,* Cambridge, 1962

—— *The Historian and Character,* Cambridge, 1963

J. C. Morrison, *Life and Times of St Bernard of Clairvaux,* London, 1863

C. P. M. Sabatier, *St Francis of Assisi,* Hodder and Stoughton, 1894

F. G. Sitwell, *St Odo of Cluny,* Sheed and Ward, 1958

7 Schools and Scholars

C. H. Haskins, *The Rise of the Universities,* New York, 1923

—— *Studies in Medieval Culture,* Oxford, 1929

—— *The Rennaissance of the Twelfth Century,* New York, 1957

H. P. Lattin, Peasant Boy (a simply written life of Gerbert), New York, 1951

—— *Gerbert's Letters,* Columbia Records, 1961

D. D. McGarry (tr.), *Letters of John of Salisbury,* Nelson's Medieval Texts

—— *The Metalogicon of John of Salisbury*, Cambridge, 1955
R. L. Poole, *Illustrations of the History of Medieval Thought*, New York, 1960
H. Rashdall (Ed. F. Powicke and A. Emden), *The Universities of Europe in the Middle Ages* (Vol. III), Oxford, 1936
Helen Waddell, *The Wandering Scholars*, Pelican, 1954
F. A. Yeldham, *The Story of Reckoning in the Middle Ages*, Harrap, 1926

8 Church Builders and Artists

J. Beckwith, *Early Medieval Art*, Thames and Hudson, 1964
G. G. Coulton, *Art and the Reformation*, Oxford, 1928
Joan Evans, *Art in Medieval France*, Oxford, 1948
D. C. Grivot and G. Zarnecki, *Gislebertus*, Collins, 1961
D. Knoop and D. P. Jones, *The Medieval Mason*, Manchester, 1966
J. B. A. Lassus and R. Willis (Ed.), *The Album of Villars de Honnecourt*, London, 1858
W. R. Lethaby (revised by D. Talbot Rice), *Medieval Art*, Nelson, 1949
Émile Mâle, *The Gothic Image*, Fontana Library, 1961
E. Panofsky (tr.), *Abbot Suger*, Princeton, 1946
Theophilus (C. R. Dodwell, tr.), *De Diversis Artibus*, Nelson, 1961

9 Doctors and Patients

J. M. W. Bean, *Plague in the Later Middle Ages*, The Economic History Review, Second Series (Vol. XV), No. 3, 1963
Boccaccio (J. M. Rigg, tr.), *The Decameron*, Angus and Robertson, 1954
Anna Campbell, *The Black Death and Men of Learning*, New York, 1931
Cardinal F. A. Gasquet, *The Great Pestilence*, 1348–9, London, 1893
L. Fabian Hirst, *The Conquest of Plague*, Oxford, 1953
Brian Inglis, *History of Medicine*, Weidenfeld and Nicolson, 1965
Loren C. McKinney, *Early Medieval Medicine*, John Hopkins University, Baltimore, 1937
J. H. Mundy, *Essays in Medieval Life and Thought*, Nelson, 1955
C. Singer and Henry Sigerist (Ed.), *Essays on the History of Medicine*, Oxford, 1924
Lynn Thorndike, *Science and Thought in the Fifteenth Century*, New York, 1929

10 Scientists and Technologists

Agnes Arber, *Herbals*, Cambridge, 1966

R. W. T. Gunther, *The Herbal of Apuleius*, Roxburghe Club, 1925

C. L. Haskins, *Studies in the History of Medieval Science*, Harvard, 1924

Dard Hunter, *Papermaking*, Pleiades Books, 1947

G. H. T. Kimble, *Geography in the Middle Ages*, Methuen, 1938

J. Read, *Prelude to Chemistry*, Bell, 1936

G. A. L. Sarton, *Introduction to the History of Science* (3 Vols.), Washington, 1927–48

Charles Singer, *A Short History of Science*, Oxford, 1949

—— *A History of Technology* (Vol. 2), Oxford, 1956

Lynn Thorndike, *The Herbal of Rufinus*, Medieval Academy of America and University of Chicago, 1946

INDEX

Numerals in **bold type** refer to illustration numbers.

If you have enjoyed this book you may also like these

THE STORY OF MAUDE REED *by Norah Lofts* 25p
552 52010 1 Carousel Fiction

Her grandfather was only a wool merchant and his house was not considered suitable for a young girl of noble blood. Maude was now old enough to be taught the accomplishments of a lady: sewing, music and the art of graceful behaviour. But this was the Fifteenth Century, and her school was to be an old, dark castle.

THE CLASHING ROCKS *by Ian Serraillier* 20p
552 52022 5

Ian Serraillier tells the story of Jason and the Argonauts, and of their quest in search of the golden fleece. Jason and his crew sailed from Thessaly to the Black Sea, encountering many of the daunting figures from Greek mythology. This is the world of classical Greece, full of demons and gods, and in Ian Serraillier's hands the timeless story is both a great myth and a gripping adventure story.

THE STORY OF BRITAIN *by R. J. Unstead* 30p
Series Carousel Non-Fiction

A country is forged by its history, the battles and intrigues of by-gone ages laying the foundations of today. From its beginnings as an island to the end of the Second World War, this series is the record of the men and women who played a role in shaping the character of England now. It traces the emergence of England as a nation.

THE MODEL-RAILWAY MEN *by Ray Pope*   25p
552 52024 1

Mark operates his model railway as near to the real thing as possible. Then he encounters the Telford family, miniature people who live only for the railway – Mark's railway. The adventures of Mark and his live passengers will be enjoyed by anyone who has known the delights of a model railway.

RICH AND FAMOUS AND BAD *by Rodie Sudbury*   30p
552 52027 6

Polly and Judith scorned their classmates' interest in boys. They preferred Judith's brother and his friends to keep out of their way. Then Judith's feelings changed – and Polly invented the kind of boy she would like to know. But soon she finds her fantasy world turning into a frightening reality, and her daydream of being 'rich, famous and bad' turns into a nightmare.

THEFT *by Wendy Robertson*   25p
552 52025 X

In a working class town in the North, three young children find some books and gold coins in a shed behind the local pub. They take them, but soon their conscience makes them return their find. And when they do so, they witness a real robbery, which poses a problem: 'We couldn't get help 'cos the cops would be asking what we were doing out here in the middle of the night.'

ROYAL ADVENTURERS *by R. J. Unstead*　　　　25p
552 54018 8

R. J. Unstead, the top children's historian, writes in ROYAL ADVENTURERS that kings and queens are 'more powerful, more generous, foolish or cruel than the rest of mankind.' He then delves into both the careers and personalities of a variety of regal figures, from Julius Caesar and Genghis Khan to Charlemagne and Marie Antoinette.

THE BOOK OF EXPERIMENTS *by Leonard de Vries*　30p
552 54020 X

Would you like to become an inventor? This book will show you how. Would you like to experience the adventure of scientific discovery in your own home? This book offers 150 such experiments which can be done safely and at little or no cost – for example, with nails you can make either a piano or an electric motor. Many equally amazing discoveries await the reader of this book.

**THE HOW AND WHY WONDER BOOK OF
EXTINCT ANIMALS**　　　　25p
552 86555 9

Here is a fabulous array of animals that have become extinct, from the early dinosaurs to more recent victims of man's actions. And there is also a warning: many species including pandas, tigers and leopards are in danger of disappearing, and the final question posed is 'Is the human race becoming extinct?'

LOOKING AND FINDING *by Geoffrey Grigson*   25p

552 54007 2   Carousel Non-Fiction

You can find sunken treasure, hidden away in some long-forgotten shipwreck, or discover the past through scattered fossils and ancient inscriptions. It depends what you're looking for, how you go about finding it. It depends where you're looking, how you go about getting there. But once the search begins, there's no knowing what you might stumble across.

THE STORY OF JODRELL BANK *by Roger Piper*   30p

552 54028 5

We now live in the space age, and Jodrell Bank stands as one of the greatest achievements of stellar technology. Here is the whole story of the 'Big Dish', including its history, how it works, and some of the amazing facts discovered by this modern wonder of the world. Also included are eight pages of photographs.

THE HOW AND WHY WONDER BOOK OF
THE TOWER OF LONDON   20p

552 86545 1

The Tower of London is one of Britain's most famous historical buildings. Today it is known for the crown jewels and the world-famous 'Beefeaters'. In the past it has housed Kings and Queens, and served as a prison for Sir Walter Raleigh, the 'Little Princes', and other well-known people. The full story of the Tower's past and present is retold in this book, with many illustrations.

These books are available at bookshops and newsagents. If you have difficulty finding them you can buy them by post from the following address:

Transworld Publishers Ltd., P.O. Box 11, Falmouth, Cornwall. Please send with your order a cheque or postal order (not currency) to cover the cost of the book, plus 6p for each book ordered to cover the cost of postage and packing.